ואביא אתכם אלי

I Brought You unto Me

ואביא אתכם אלי

I Brought You unto Me

A FRESH LOOK AT MA'AMAD HAR SINAI

AND

THE ASERES HADIBROS

MOSHE M. EISEMANN

Rabbi Moshe M. Eisemann
403 Yeshiva Lane, Apt. 1B
Baltimore, MD 21208
(410) 484-7396

www.kishinievyeshiva.org

Designed by Misha Beletsky

Edited by Sara Eisemann

This book was set in
Adobe Brioso Pro and Narkiss Classic MFO

ISBN 978-0-9817642-0-7

10 9 8 7 6 5 4 3 2 1

DISTRIBUTED BY:
Feldheim Publishers
POB 35002, Jerusalem, Israel 91350
200 Airport Executive Park, Nanuet, NY 10954
www.feldheim.com

Printed in the USA

CONTENTS

בס"ד

RABBI AHARON FELDMAN

ROSH HAYESHIVA

NER ISRAEL RABBINICAL COLLEGE

STUDY: 400 MT. WILSON LANE (410) 484-7200

RESIDENCE: 409 YESHIVA LANE (410) 653-9433

FAX (410) 484-3060

BALTIMORE, MARYLAND 21208

פורים דמוקפין תשס"ח

Rabbi Eisemann has deeply influenced the students at Ner Yisroel with his classes for over thirty years. It is therefore a matter of great joy for me to learn that he is now disseminating his teachings in book form where they will be available to the general public.

From the essays I have seen it is clear that they are inspiring and incisive in their analysis of their respective topics, as well as beautifully presented through elegant and masterful writing.

It is my hope that this book will be well received by all lovers of Torah learning and that it will be given all the recognition which it truly deserves.

With respects,

Aharon Feldman

Aharon Feldman
Rosh Yeshivas Ner Yisroel
Baltimore, MD

PREFACE

A Look at Where We Are Headed

R Simchah Zisel (the Alter of Kelm) was not only a great *Baal Musar*; he was also a peerless educator. For a number of years he ran a Yeshiva in Grubin for promising youngsters who, for all their superior minds, needed to learn how to learn. He was most particular about whom he would hire as a teacher. It was not enough for someone to have a good grasp of the subject and the ability to hold the students' interest. The applicant had to agree to adopt the methodology that the Alter had developed. He had very specific ideas about how a complicated *Tosafos* was to be taught. Among them was his insistence that the Rebbe not simply begin reading the *Tosafos,* translating and explaining as he went along. The entire *Tosafos* had to be mapped out and explained to the students *orally,* long before the text was ever approached. At each stage the students had to know ahead of time precisely what was about to happen and where *Tosafos* would now be heading. Absent such oral preparation, the class would remain so many blobs of confusion.[1]

I tell this little story in order to help you understand the purpose of this Preface. Friends who have read the book in manuscript have warned me that there are sections that are quite complicated. They darkly predicted dire consequences. I would lose readers who might have neither the time nor the inclination to plow through it all. Believe me, when an author hears that, he listens. I certainly do not want to lose readers and ideally I would like everybody who picks up this book to enjoy reading it and to feel that he has gained something significant.

Because of this, I have decided to follow the Alter's advice. Right here, before you even begin reading the book, I will tell you what it is all about: why I wrote it, what its thesis is, and where it will all end. That way, as you move from chapter to chapter, you will have a reasonably clear sense of where we are going and how we intend to get there.

So what is this book all about?

From the very beginning, it has been my companion on my personal odyssey in search of a better understanding of Shavuos. The other Yamim Tovim were not a problem to me; their messages were crisp and clear; I felt confident in gauging what they demanded of me. Shavuos seemed fuzzy. I always assumed that it was a time for celebrating the Torah, that sweet and precious gift that the Ribono shel Olam had made to us on that day.[2] However, as I started thinking about it, I developed a nagging feeling that something was not quite right. Shavuos is the anniversary of *Ma'amad Har Sinai* and at Har Sinai we heard only *Aseres HaDibros,* not the whole Torah.[3] Even these were not really "given" to us until after they had been inscribed upon the *luchos* and handed by the Ribono shel Olam to Moshe Rabbeinu.[4]

Then there are *Aseres HaDibros,* the ten *Dibros* that we were told on that day. For years I was unable to discover the nature of this tensome.[5] I, like most other people, knew that these ten *Dibros* could be considered as general categories (*Avos*) under which all other *mitzvos* could be subsumed and that, further, they were divisible into two sections, one defining our relationship with the Ribono shel Olam, the other with our fellow humans.[6] However, although obviously true, this left me unsatisfied. I reasoned that if the entire exercise revolved around the "*Avos* nature" of these ten *Dibros* and the fact that they comprised obligations both to God and to man, the laws of economy should have determined that just two *mitzvos* could have served as well as do the ten. The Ribono shel Olam might have chosen the first *Dibra* as the *Av* for the former, and, as did Hillel,[7] the obligation to love our fellow as we love ourselves[8] for the latter. There seemed to me to be a lot of wastage here.

Furthermore, I was unable to find satisfying explanations as to why the particular *mitzvos* that appear in *Aseres HaDibros,* rather than any others, should have been considered as *Avos.* Why choose honoring our parents rather than fearing them (VaYikra 19:3)? Why does stealing a person (surely a very rare occurrence) make the grade as the eighth *Dibra* (Sanhedrin 86a) rather than stealing an object?

More research seemed to be in order. I tried hard to get to

the sources and form some kind of opinion, and, as I am wrapping up the book and slowly moving toward publication, I feel a modest sense of accomplishment. I have discovered a great deal that I did not know before and have been able to develop a thesis that feels satisfying.

My thesis has its genesis in a single remark that Ramban makes in his Chumash commentary to Yisro where *Ma'amad Har Sinai* is first described. Once the idea began to germinate, I found much confirmation for it throughout the Ramban commentary to Chumash and I feel that, at the very least, it is worthy of serious consideration. Of course in this Preface there is no place for identifying the various sources that I marshaled, but I will tell you what the thesis is.

It suggests that the revelation of *Aseres HaDibros* from atop Mount Sinai was no more than a part of a much larger drama. What we are celebrating on Shavuos is a Chasunah, a wedding consecrated between the Ribono shel Olam and ourselves (see Ta'anis 26b).[9] Shavuos is a day of unbounded elation and happiness for both Chasan and Kallah, a forming of a new entity, a fusion and a oneness established between the Ribono shel Olam and ourselves. It is a wonderful match that, for all the buffeting and knocks that can test even the best of marriages—particularly those lasting thousands of years—will last and be a blessing for all eternity. On Shavuos we have a lot to be dancing about.

In this marriage *Aseres HaDibros,* once they were engraved upon the *luchos,* became the wedding ring. They constituted the formal handing over of an earnest to everlasting commitment.[10]

So much for what actually happened. But, as we asked earlier, we still have to find out what was so special about these particular *mitzvos.* While, once more, the details do not belong in a Preface, the simple unadorned answer does. It is this: A nation so closely tied to the Ribono shel Olam has to maintain an extremely high standard of purity and probity. As the Torah tells us in the Yisro passage, they must become a *Mamleches Kohanim VeGoy Kadosh. Aseres HaDibros,* beyond their standing as ordinary *mitzvos,* are a listing of the constitutional principles to which we must adhere and by which we must shape our lives if we are to live up to the responsibilities that our lofty standing imposes upon us. We have devoted eleven chapters, chapters 9–19, to examining each one of the *Dibros* to learn what values lie hidden under their ordinary *mitzvah* standing.

I believe that what I have now written about the *Aseres HaDibros* is expressed by the Rambam in his Mishnah commentary to Tamid 5:1. That Mishnah teaches that as a part of the Morning Service as it was performed in Beis HaMikdash, *Aseres HaDibros* were read every day just before Shema. The Rambam explains that this custom developed because these ten *Dibros* are *the basis for all the mitzvos and the place from which they start.*[11] I cannot think of any meaning for these words other than what I have suggested in the previous paragraph.

I have given this book the title ואביא אתכם אלי, *I Brought You unto Me,* because that is how the Ribono shel Olam Himself described the purpose of having brought us to Sinai (Shemos 19:4). The plagues with which He had smitten the Egyptians, the "eagle's wings" with which He had outfitted us to speed us on our way, really all of the history through which our family had passed since Avraham first took up the wanderer's staff, all had only this one purpose. We were on our way to our Chasunah—and now we had arrived (Ta'anis 26b). And, as at a true Chasunah, the ring that the Chasan gives his Kallah is less central than the staggering fact that two disparate humans had now pledged themselves to become one indivisible entity (Bereishis 2:24). The big story of *Ma'amad Har Sinai* is the union that the Ribono shel Olam forged with us. The handing down of *Aseres HaDibros* is only a part.

I suppose that I could sum up my thesis by using *Birkas HaTorah* as a model. *Who has chosen us from among the nations and given us His Torah.* The Ribono shel Olam gave us His Torah because He had chosen us; He had made us into His bride, and because we were His bride He entrusted us with *Aseres HaDibros.* That, I think, says it all. And that is the subject of the small book that I am now offering to you.

So, when next Shavuos comes around, I suggest that besides celebrating the day by learning as much as we can—and maybe a little more—we also take the time to rejoice in who we are and in the kind of relationship that the Ribono shel Olam forged with us. Let us recall that the Ribono shel Olam did not say that He brought us to Sinai so that He would be able to give us *Aseres HaDibros* there. What He did say was

ואביא אתכם אלי

Both Emor (VaYikra 23:15-22) and Re'eih (Devarim 16:9–12) present Shavuos unambiguously and unabashedly as a harvest festival with never a hint that it might have anything more sacred than a combine harvester in mind.[12] On the other hand, the fact that this Yom Tov is celebrated on the fiftieth day of the *Omer,* after counting seven days seven times for a total of seven weeks,[13] is so reminiscent of the holiest moment in the Jewish calendar, the Yovel, the fiftieth year that comes to us after counting seven years seven times for a total of seven *shemitos,* that there can be no doubt at all that among the Yamim Tovim, Shavuos is the Holy of Holies. Clearly there is something here that requires a great deal of thought.

I know where to go for a solution. The story of Moshe Rabbeinu's encounter with the Ribono shel Olam at the burning bush, learned as Ramban learned it, slowly, carefully, and lovingly, can yield some very profound ideas.

So let us just remind ourselves of some of the details that made up the story. Moshe Rabbeinu is shepherding Yisro's flock and comes to Chorev, to the foot of the very mountain that later we will meet as Har Sinai. As he approaches the mountain he sees that, at its peak, a bush is burning but is not being consumed by the flames. Moshe, intrigued by this strange sight, decides to approach the bush to see what might be the explanation of its resilience. As he draws closer, he hears the Ribono shel Olam's voice calling to him from within the flames, commanding him to take off his shoes since he is standing on holy ground.

At this point Ramban makes his first observation. Moshe

Rabbeinu was presumably still quite far removed from the bush. Why should the shoes be a problem at that distance? His answer is shattering in its simplicity—and in its significance. What is happening here, claims Ramban, is precisely what would happen later at *Ma'amad Har Sinai*. There, although the Shechinah was ensconced atop the mountain, the *entire* mountain was placed out of bounds for everyone because all of it became holy; here too the same principle was at work. It is true that the bush was far removed, at the top of the mountain. Nevertheless, the Ribono shel Olam's presence sanctified the whole mountain.

This is the first indication of the sheer breadth of Ramban's unfettered vision. He will come back to it several times in the various *pesukim* that describe the drama of that occasion. Moshe Rabbeinu standing before the burning bush was a mini *Ma'amad Har Sinai*! He lived through precisely that which the entire people would experience later.

The story continues and the Ribono shel Olam apprises Moshe Rabbeinu of His plan. Moshe would go to Pharaoh, force the emancipation of His people, and, that done, would lead them to Canaan, the land that He had promised to the Avos.

Ramban and Rashi disagree on practically every word in the following conversation between the Ribono shel Olam and Moshe Rabbeinu. We will be following Ramban. It would take too long to delineate the various points upon which Rashi and he disagree, though it is a very rewarding *sugia* to learn. If you do decide to follow it up, I would advise you to have the Beis HaYayin commentary on the Ramban beside you. It will help a great deal in deciphering all of the complexities.

So here we go with Ramban's presentation of what happened. Moshe Rabbeinu protests. He argues that, even if the Jews would accept his leadership to the extent that they would follow him out of Egypt, they would never agree to have him take them to Canaan. They knew all about the mighty warriors who lived there and would certainly balk at the prospect of having to fight them. His assigned task, Moshe Rabbeinu protested, was beyond him.

The Ribono shel Olam had a ready answer. "Get them to go with you to Sinai. That part of the assignment will go easily. Once they will have experienced *Ma'amad Har Sinai,* once they will have subordinated themselves to My will, a great change will have come over them. They will not hesitate to follow you wherever you will lead."

This is a bare-bones synopsis of how Ramban reads the part of the story that concerns us.

Here is a big question that, as far as I can make out, Ramban does not address directly. Still, his commentary, as I have paraphrased it here, demands that it be asked. Why was it necessary to have Moshe Rabbeinu experience a mini-*Ma'amad Har Sinai*? Throughout his life, the Ribono shel Olam would be communicating with him, but never from within a burning bush. Why did the Sinaitic flames have to rage for him on this occasion?

They had to rage because the idea that Moshe Rabbeinu was experiencing, precisely that which all of us would be living through later, lies at the very center of Ramban's reading of this *sugia*. The issue at stake in Moshe Rabbeinu's argument with God was whether or not people could change. Moshe's point was that the people were deathly afraid; that they would *never* agree to battle the Canaanite giants. The Ribono shel Olam counters that Sinai's fire is a transforming, not a consuming, one. Bring them to Sinai and you will see that their view of what is and what is not possible will change quickly enough. Moshe could test this proposition by his own experience right here and now. Was not his own life, his own sense of worth, his very being, changed by the fire that roared in the bush? The same would happen to his people.

I will tell you why I think that that I am on the right track in the explanation that I just offered. It is because, if I am wrong, there would be a glaring problem in the *p'shuto shel mikra* that Ramban does not seem to address. It is this. As soon as Moshe Rabbeinu noticed that the bush was not being consumed, he reacted as he should have done. He asked a question: Why should the bush not be consumed? It is a great question. What is the answer?[14]

Nowhere in this *parshah* does Ramban make any effort to find the solution for this problem in the text. That can only be understood if the Torah itself gives the answer. It is this: The vision at the bush was granted to him for only this one purpose. He had to learn that there are fires and fires. There are those that destroy and those that transform. Sinai's fires are life-altering and in their heat a *Mamleches Kohanim VeGoy Kadosh* would be born. This was the lesson that Moshe Rabbeinu needed to learn if he was to believe in his own mission. Moshe Rabbeinu's question about the bush's resilience was answered as soon as his mission was revealed to him. It made sense only against the background of what the fire and the bush had taught him.

Do you remember what started us on this long trip? It was our surprise at the Torah's presentation of Shavuos. Is it crassly physical or is it sublimely holy? The answer is, of course, that it is the story of the crassly physical being sublimated by the sublimely holy. It is the story of *Ma'amad Har Sinai* and its cleansing flames. At Sinai the Ribono shel Olam *kashered* a slave people and made it into a *Mamleches Kohanim VeGoy Kadosh*. That is what we celebrate on Shavuos.

The perceptive reader will long ago have understood what I am getting at. The story of the burning bush understood as a forerunner of *Ma'amad Har Sinai* defines *Ma'amad Har Sinai* in precisely those terms that I have suggested in this Preface and throughout this book. It is a story of sublimation, of turning dross into gold, of elevating a fairly ordinary people into the Ribono shel Olam's *segulah*. It is, in short, a story that can be encapsulated into the three words that constitute the title of this book:

ואביא אתכם אלי

I have a question.

I cannot say that it has been bothering me for years because, truth to tell, it has not. To be totally honest, I just thought of it as I was wondering how to begin this book. You, dear Reader, will appreciate that the opening sentence is always the hardest one to compose. How do you start? How do you introduce yourself to a skeptical reader and convince him that it is worth his while to spend some time with you? How do you whet his appetite? How do you reassure him that he will not be bored, nor patronized, nor inveigled into contemplation of abstruse issues that will leave him uninformed?

So beginnings are important and that is why I want to share this question with you.

Many siddurim list *shesh zechiros,*[1] six fundamental beliefs that we as Jews are called upon to remember daily.[2] *Yetzi'as Mitzrayim* is the first of these[3]; *Ma'amad Har Sinai* is the second.[4] The other four do not concern us in the present context.

Here is my question. Our Jewish life is punctuated by all manner of *mitzvos* designed to remind us of *Yetzi'as Mitzrayim.*[5] We need only think of our twice-daily *Shema* in which the third paragraph is specifically devoted to just this remembrance. There are of course many, many more. However, to the best of my knowledge there is not a single *mitzvah* that has the purpose of reminding us of *Ma'amad Har Sinai.* Why not? Surely it is not a matter of one *zechirah* being somehow more important than another.[6]

In a way, this entire book constitutes an attempt to explain why things are as they are. However, like an accordion, the answer that I feel to be the true one can be contracted or expanded. It can be stated in a few brief, businesslike sentences or, if we can open our hearts wide enough, those sentences can swell and encompass infinity. They have room for large expanses of passionate feelings, of love and caring for the Ribono shel Olam. And it does not stop there. That same love, that same caring can be focused upon our fellow Jews, all of them, really all of them. If we do not know them now, we knew them once, for we rubbed shoulders with them at Sinai. Do we not, at some level, recall the time when we all trembled together at the foot of that ominous mountain? And, trembling together, we all became melded by roaring thunder and flashing lightning, into one eternal and indivisible whole?

Come. Let us get to know each other a little better.

ONE

Some Challenging Questions

You and I, dear Reader, are going to have to flex our intellectual muscles. Chazal teach us that reexamining the old comes much harder than learning something new.[1]

That is so because we have a vested interest in leaving good enough alone. Casting a critical eye upon well-known and well-loved platitudes will only force us into a battle that we cannot win. Why put ourselves into a position in which we will have to admit that until now we have been satisfied with the shallow and the non-demanding? Who needs the headache?

But you know, dear Reader, the mere fact that you are continuing to read marks you as a stouthearted optimist. You may know from experience, or if you do not, you at least intuit, the boundless sweetness in which newfound clarity and understanding comes packaged. You may know, or if you do not, you intuit that in self-abnegation lies self-affirmation, that the one possession that nobody can ever take away from you is that knowledge that, by your effort and your determination, you wrested from the abyss of ignorance in which we all initially flounder.

I will tell you how I know all this. It all happened to me in the last few days. I have passed through valleys of despondency when I realized that after many, many years of learning I am still woefully ignorant of some of the most basic components of *yiddishkeit*. But I came out at the other end. I worked hard and made some discoveries. I am less ignorant now than I was before. There is a lot of joy in that.

Enough said. Let us get to work.

In this initial essay, our interest will focus upon the introduction that the Ribono shel Olam gave to Moshe Rabbeinu when we first arrived at Sinai (Shemos 19:3–6).[2] Let us see what was actually said and then we will get to the exciting part, the analysis that will give us a better understanding of what truly happened in those packed and portentous six days.

ג. ...כה תאמר לבית יעקב ותגיד לבני ישראל.
ד. אתם ראיתם אשר עשיתי למצרים ואשא אתכם על כנפי נשרים ואבא אתכם אלי.
ה. ועתה אם שמוע תשמעו בקלי ושמרתם את בריתי והייתם לי סגלה מכל העמים כי לי כל הארץ.
ו. ואתם תהיו לי ממלכת כהנים וגוי קדוש ...(שמות פרק י"ט)

3. ... "Thus shall you speak to Beis Yaakov and tell it to the B'nei Yisrael.
4. 'You yourselves witnessed what I did to Egypt and that [after that I] carried you upon eagles' wings and brought you unto Me.
5. Now, if you will listen carefully to My voice and will be true to My covenant, you shall become My very own possession [chosen] from among all the nations....
6. Then you will become a Kingdom of Kohanim and a Holy People unto Me.'"

We will use the remainder of the present chapter to scan these four verses and see what issues seem to require explanation. After we have done that, we will be able to take our time. Sometimes we will be able to go straight to the issue at hand; occasionally a more roundabout route may be required. I cannot promise that we will be able to tackle the problems in the order in which we raise them. It lies in the nature of learning Torah that, far from being able to impose solutions upon recalcitrant subject matter, we must hope and pray that the solutions will seek us out and lovingly offer themselves to us, often when we least expect them. I hope that by the end of the book, we will be able to feel confident that all the subjects we raise here will have been addressed. I promise you that there will be enough to keep us busy.

We begin with verse 3. *Thus shall you speak to Beis Yaakov and tell it to the B'nei Yisrael.* I would like to understand why we, the Jewish people, are divided into *Beis Yaakov* and *B'nei Yisrael.* We all know the famous Rashi that *Beis Yaakov* refers to the women, and *B'nei Yisrael* to the men. Ramban, at least on this *pasuk,* is silent. Nevertheless, I have a feeling that Ramban disagrees with Rashi.

We need very much to get this straight. It matters, indeed it matters profoundly, how the Ribono shel Olam looked upon us at this pivotal moment. Let us think this through together.

Before anything else, let us lay down the ground rules that will govern our research. It is a truism that in the Ribono shel Olam's Torah, nothing appears in the text without a purpose and, even if the purpose is clear, it will only appear at the specific place where it is absolutely required if it is to accomplish its function.[3] If you have taken the time to glance at note 3, you will surely agree that this is so.

Let us then put Rashi's interpretation to the test. The Ribono shel Olam wants Moshe Rabbeinu to realize that the best way to teach women is not identical to the method that is appropriate for men. The approach to men should be businesslike and sharp. Things are to be taught as they are, including the punishments that will follow upon an infraction and all the many details that are required if the total picture is to be grasped. Women require a softer, gentler tone. No need to trouble them with threats of punishment for dereliction. No need to pile on all the stringencies that, under varying circumstances, might be involved.[4]

That is clear enough. But why now? Why before anything else? On this first day, in this first communication, there is not even a hint of commandments to follow, which might involve punishments if they are not fulfilled punctiliously. Where, amid the call for being true to the Ribono shel Olam's covenant and readying oneself to become part of a Kingdom of Kohanim and a Nation Cleaving to Him Who is Holy[5] are the many details which would weigh down upon the women? The pedagogical message is no doubt important and would, when the time comes to teach the *mitzvos,* have to be conveyed to Moshe Rabbeinu. But why now, before it is of any practical application?

It is for this reason that I suspect that even Rashi might agree that the Midrashic interpretation that he cites is not the *p'shuto shel mikra,* the simple meaning of the phrase.

I mentioned earlier that Ramban offers no interpretation for these two expressions. However, I know of two other places where his remarks might shed light upon how he reads our passage. The first is close by, right here in our neighborhood. In verse 1 we have a phrase that tells us that after Klal Yisrael reached Midbar Sin, *Yisrael camped over against the mountain*. Ramban is troubled by the seemingly superfluous word "Yisrael." He suggests that the wording is meant to convey that only "Yisrael," only those who were Jewish by birth, camped immediately in front of the mountain. The *erev rav,* the Egyptians who had decided to throw in their lot with the Jews, were camped further back. Ramban reasons as follows: "for the Torah was to be given only to the Jews, as it is written, "Thus shall you speak to Beis Yaakov and tell it to the B'nei Yisrael."

From this wording it would appear that Ramban takes the combination Yaakov/Yisrael as the Ribono shel Olam's way of describing the Jewish people in its narrowest sense, that is, with even proselytes excluded. The idea that Klal Yisrael might be regarded as a composite made up of "Yaakov" and "Yisrael" certainly does not derive from the fact that one of the names stands for women and the other for men. Every nation is constituted of both males and females. It must be that these two names convey the idea that the Jewish people have a unique mix of characteristics. There are some that can be traced to the "Yaakov" aspect that was lodged in the third Patriarch, and others that belong to the "Yisrael" within him.[6]

This is borne out by the Ramban to BeMidbar 23:9. There Bil'am praises Klal Yisrael as a people that *dwells alone*. Ramban explains: Israel will never blend comfortably into the family of nations. They have standards that are not compatible with those of other people—they dwell alone *under the names of Yaakov and Yisrael.*[7]

Clearly, in this context, Yisrael and Yaakov do not stand for men and women.[8]

We have reached the point at which we can reiterate the question that we asked above. Why, in the present context, is it appropriate to assign the two names, Yaakov and Yisrael, to the Jewish people?

This brings us to the end of our problems with verse 3.

From the point of view of its content, verse 4 is unproblematic. The message of love and caring that it conveys could not be clearer. If there is a problem, it is one of "Why?" not one of "What?" Why mention this here? Why would this have any bearing upon *Ma'amad Har Sinai*?[9] The answer is not obvious and we must live with the fact that we will not understand verse 4 correctly until we win a better understanding of what was about to happen.[10]

The issues with verse 5 are more complex. The verse contains three subjects: we are to listen carefully to God's voice; we are to be true to His covenant; and this will result in our becoming God's *segulah*. Each of these ideas will require our definition. What, in the first phrase, is God's voice telling us? Which covenant does the second phrase have in mind?[11] What exactly is the *segulah* that we are to become?

Verse 6 is very much like verse 4. There is nothing particularly difficult with any of the terms, but we will not fully grasp what is being said until we understand more precisely what the entire passage is meant to convey.[12]

We are going to be very busy throughout this book. Come, let us stride on together. Clarity lies at the end of the search and clarity is worth pursuing. May the Ribono shel Olam guide us along our path.

TWO

And You Will Be True to My Covenant

As I think back to the ground we covered in the previous chapter, it occurs to me that the many questions that we asked, and for which I promised an attempt to find answers, can really be expressed as a function of a central unknown. What exactly was the purpose of *Ma'amad Har Sinai*? Why was it needed?[1] What did it accomplish? Once we have an answer to that, everything ought to fall into place.

Ma'amad Har Sinai was of course the most profoundly determinative event in our history. Everything that happened before was only in preparation for that watershed moment.[2] If we are to understand ourselves as individuals and as a people, we must first understand what *Ma'amad Har Sinai* accomplished. Verse 6 in the Yisro passage that we began to examine in the previous chapter tells us that this experience was meant to turn us into a very special kind of nation. We are to become a *Mamleches Kohanim VeGoy Kadosh*. We must assume that the Torah will not leave us in the dark about the implications of our selection to this hugely responsible role. Once we know those, it seems likely that we will have a better understanding for why the experience was necessary.

So this is our agenda. We want to subject the Torah's account of *Matan Torah* to very careful scrutiny to see whether we can uncover some of its secrets, and use what we will have learned to plumb the mystery of our being and our destiny.

Come, let us begin our explorations.

I am persuaded that the crucial verse among the four that we listed in chapter 1 is the third one, verse 5. It is the one that calls upon us to *listen carefully*[3] to God's *voice* and to *be true to* His *covenant*. To which "voice" are we adjured to listen; to which "covenant" are we adjured to be true? If we can find the answers to these two questions, we will have cleared the first obstacle on our path to understanding.

We will first see if we can identify the covenant (*bris*) that is meant in this context. That is the simplest route to go since both Rashi and Ramban have an opinion, while neither offers anything for "voice" (*kol*). We will take up the question of the *kol* in the next chapter.

The far-reaching differences between Rashi and the Ramban that we will encounter throughout this book are grounded in two vastly different interpretations of the *bris* to which we were asked to be true. We will have to go very carefully here.

EXCURSUS

At the end of *parashas* Mishpatim, the Torah describes a covenant that was forged between the Ribono shel Olam and us in conjunction with *Matan Torah*.

I will present the text of that passage here. For the purpose of our discussions in these essays, it is not necessary to enter into a detailed analysis. Suffice it to say that Rashi and Ramban differ widely concerning the timing of this event and the text of the "Sefer HaBris" that Moshe Rabbeinu read to the people as part of this ceremony. These disagreements have no bearing upon our interest in this *parshah*. They are distinct from their disagreement about the Yisro *bris*.

This *bris* is relevant to our discussion since, in the view of most commentators, God's insistence (in our verse 5) that we remain true to the covenant He made with us refers to this Mishpatim *bris*. As we shall see, Ramban stands alone in interpreting the Yisro *bris* as referring to a different covenant.

Here is the Mishpatim passage.

א. ואל משה אמר עלה אל יהוה אתה ואהרן נדב ואביהוא ושבעים מזקני ישראל והשתחויתם מרחק.
ב. ונגש משה לבדו אל יהוה והם לא יגשו והעם לא יעלו עמו.
ג. ויבא משה ויספר לעם את כל דברי יהוה ואת כל המשפטים ויען כל העם קול אחד ויאמרו כל הדברים אשר דבר יהוה נעשה.
ד. ויכתב משה את כל דברי יהוה וישכם בבקר ויבן מזבח תחת ההר ושתים עשרה מצבה לשנים עשר שבטי ישראל.
ה. וישלח את נערי בני ישראל ויעלו עלת ויזבחו זבחים שלמים ליהוה פרים.

ו. ויקח משה חצי הדם וישם באגנת וחצי הדם זרק על המזבח.
ז. ויקח ספר הברית ויקרא באזני העם ויאמרו כל אשר דבר יהוה נעשה ונשמע.
ח. ויקח משה את הדם ויזרק על העם ויאמר הנה דם הברית אשר כרת יהוה עמכם על כל הדברים האלה.

1. To Moshe He said, "Go up to HaShem, you and Aaron, Nadav and Avihu, together with seventy of Israel's elders and prostrate yourselves from a distance.
2. Then Moshe alone should draw near to HaShem, but they should not draw near. Moreover, the people should not go up with him.
3. Moshe came and told the people all that God had said, together with all the laws. Then the people, with one voice, said, "All that God has spoken we shall do!"
4. Then Moshe wrote all the words of HaShem, rose up early in the morning, built an altar beneath the mountain together with twelve pillars that paralleled the twelve tribes of Israel.
5. He then sent the young men of Israel to sacrifice to HaShem burned offerings and other sacrifices, bulls.
6. Then Moshe took half the blood and put it into flasks, and the other half he sprinkled upon the altar.
7. Then Moshe took the Sefer HaBris and read it to the people, who declared, "Whatever the Ribono shel Olam demands we shall do and we shall hear."
8. Then Moshe took the blood and sprinkled it upon the people, saying, "See, this is the blood of the covenant that HaShem forged with you, concerning these matters."

Let us now return to the *bris* mentioned in verse 5 of the Yisro passage. We recall that before the Excursus we were wondering which *bris* was meant in that verse. Now that we are aware of a *bris* that was forged, apparently, as part of *Matan Torah*—the Mishpatim *bris*—it seems most natural to assume that reference is to that *bris*. Here is how. We arrive at Har Sinai. In His very first communication to Moshe Rabbeinu the Ribono shel Olam adjures us to remain true to a covenant without identifying what covenant that might be. Within a few days the Ribono shel Olam will give us *Aseres HaDibros* and, apparently, as a part of that event, will forge a *bris* with us. Does it not stand to reason that this would be the *bris* mentioned immediately upon our arrival at the site?

That is, in fact, exactly what Rashi and many other commentators assume. If we scan a page of a Mikra'os Gedolos Chumash, we meet Rashi: "It is the *bris* that I will execute with you that binds you to keep the Torah."[4] Then we move over to Ibn Ezra: "That is the *bris* which I will execute with you. That refers to the *bris* that Moshe made with the Israelites after *Matan Torah* when he built the altar."[5] S'forno and Chizkuni both agree.

You, dear Reader, will certainly have noticed the absence of the Ramban in this almost unanimous lineup. The truth is that he differs, and differs profoundly, with all these commentators.

Here is what Ramban writes: AND BE TRUE TO MY COVENANT: *This refers to the covenant that I forged with your forefathers (Bereishis 17:7) to be a Lord for them and for their descendants after them.*[6] As the Ramban defines it, the Yisro covenant is not at all directly connected to keeping the Torah. It is about forging a contract with the Ribono shel Olam that He would be our God and we and all our descendants, unto all eternity, would be His people. Of course, indirectly that will involve keeping the Torah, since it is our God's wish that we do so. However, that is not the stuff of the covenant that was so urgently on the Ribono shel Olam's mind immediately upon our arrival at Sinai.

We will analyze this Ramban more closely in the coming chapters. His ideas will, in fact, become the foundation upon which the entire book will be structured. In the meanwhile we must try to understand why he seems to insist upon complicating matters. Why not take the easy route and have the *bris* refer to the most obvious one among the candidates? Why not assume that the Mishpatim *bris* was meant?

The answer surely is that in Ramban's view there was a major piece of business left dangling from the time of *Yetzi'as Mitzrayim*. This needed to be addressed now. God's insistence that we remain loyal to the covenant forged with Avraham Avinu so long ago will address it.

We recall that at the beginning of VaEira (Shemos 6:6 and 7) the Ribono shel Olam made two promises: He would free us from Egypt's slavery[7] and he would adopt us as His own very special people.[8] The first promise was fulfilled the moment that we left Egypt. Ramban teaches that the second promise would not be fulfilled until we stood at Sinai.

ולקחתי אתכם לי לעם בבואכם אל הר סיני ותקבלו התורה, כי שם נאמר (להלן יט:ה) והייתם לי סגולה.

I WILL TAKE YOU TO ME AS A NATION: That will come about when you will have arrived at Mount Sinai and accepted the Torah. For there it is written, *and [you] will be for me a* SEGULAH, *My very own possession.*

To fully appreciate what the Ramban is saying, we should look at his comments on *segulah* at Shemos 19:5.

והייתם לי סגולה מכל העמים שתהיו בידי סגולה, כדבר נחמד לא ימסרנו המלך ביד אחר, כמו וסגולת מלכים והמדינות (קהלת ב:ח). ואמר כי לי כל הארץ כטעם אשר חלק ה' אותם לכל העמים, ואתכם לקח ה' (דברים ד:יט–כ) וכך אמר ואבדיל אתכם מן העמים להיות לי (ויקרא כ:כז).

You shall be for Me a *segulah* from among all the nations: *Segulah* is a dearly beloved object owned by a king and always kept at his side. He will trust nobody at all to watch it with sufficient care. Then the verse continues, for all the earth is Mine . . . as it says, *I separated you from all the other nations that you should be Mine.*

There was something that happened at Mount Sinai other than *Matan Torah*. That something apparently needed to precede *Matan Torah*.

Matan Torah was a matter of handing down *mitzvos*[9] to the people. However, before that could reasonably have been done, a relationship had to be established that would give the Lawgiver the right to legislate for the people. The people must accept his kingship and only then can the laws that he chooses to impose upon them be binding. This is stressed again and again in Midrashim, of which the following one may be seen as representative. It is taken from Yalkut Shimoni, Shemos 6:286.

> משל למלך בשר ודם שנכנס למדינה. אמרו לו עבדיו גזור עליהם גזרות. אמר להם לכשיקבלו מלכותי אגזור עליהן גזרות שאם מלכותי אין מקבלין גזרתי היאך מקיימין. כך אמר הקב"ה לישראל אנכי ה' אלהיך לא יהיה לך אלהים אחרים אני הוא שקבלתם מלכותי עליכם במצרים. אמרו לו הן הן כשם שקבלתם מלכותי כך קבלו גזרותי לא יהיה לך אלהים אחרים. רבי שמעון בן יוחאי אומר הוא שנאמר להלן אני ה' אלהיכם כמעשה ארץ מצרים וגו' אני הוא שקבלתם מלכותי עליכם בסיני קבלו גזרותי.
>
> This is comparable to a king who came to visit a part of his kingdom. His servants begged him to give them laws. He said to them, "First accept my kingship and only then will I legislate for you, for without that, how can I expect my laws to be kept?" Thus did the Ribono shel Olam say to Yisrael, "I am HaShem your God.... You shall have no other Gods.... Am I He Whose kingship you accepted in Egypt?" They said, "Yes, yes." "If so, then just as you accepted My kingship, you are bound to live by My laws."

It seems to me that in Ramban's view the *bris* that the Ribono shel Olam mentioned in His very first communication after our arrival at Sinai referred to the requirement laid down by the Midrash that we have just quoted. Before there could be any discussion concerning the acceptance of *mitzvos,* there was the need to proclaim the Ribono shel Olam as our king and lawgiver. Our willingness to affirm the *bris* that the Ribono shel Olam had made with Avraham Avinu fulfilled that requirement.

THREE

Beginning to Consolidate Ramban's Interpretation of the Bris

In the previous chapter, we came to recognize that Ramban has introduced a dimension into the drama of *Ma'amad Har Sinai* that is absent from the offerings of the other commentators. As he reads the text, the establishment of an intimate relationship between the Ribono shel Olam and ourselves occupies a central role in those first few days of preparation to *Kabalas HaTorah.*[1]

We will now analyze this Ramban a little further.

I would like to spend a few minutes rethinking the Ramban from VaEira that we quoted at the end of the previous chapter. Let us look at it together once more and it will become clear that some more work is required.

Here is the Ramban once more.

> **ולקחתי אתכם לי לעם** בבואכם אל הר סיני **ותקבלו התורה**, כי שם נאמר (להלן יט ה) והייתם לי סגולה.
>
> I WILL TAKE YOU TO ME AS A NATION: That will come about when you will have arrived at Mount Sinai *and accepted the Torah*. For there it is written, *and [you] will be for me a* SEGULAH, *My very own possession.*

Take a good look at the Ramban. Do you have a problem? I do. It is this. Why does Ramban add the words *and accepted the Torah*? Ramban wanted to know when the Ribono shel Olam "took us as a nation." He answered that this happened at Sinai. He proved this from the fact that God speaks of our becoming His *segulah*. That should close the case. Why, in this context, mention the Torah?

Here is a possible explanation.

You will recall from chapter 2 that God laid down two conditions in verse 5. We had to agree to listen to His voice (*kol*) and we had to undertake to be true to our covenant with Him. We dealt with the question of the *bris* in that chapter. The time has now come to take up the question of the *kol.*

We have to tread softly here, because it is my feeling that we are getting close to *sisrei Torah* and, needless to say, we are not going to go where we are not wanted. So let us just note that Midrashim make an issue of the fact that the term *kol,* voice, appears seven times in our *parshah*. They further assert that the seven times that "kol" is mentioned in Tehilim 29 parallels those seven *"kolos"* (see Yalkut Shimoni, Tehilim 709).[2] Clearly things are happening here that we cannot expect to understand. Nevertheless, we are safe in concluding that the *"kol"* idea is right at the center of the Sinaitic drama.

My argument, at this point, is that given the centrality of *"kol"* in the *Ma'amad Har Sinai* narrative, it seems possible that the phrase *if you listen to My voice* (*koli*), refers specifically to *Aseres HaDibros*. I would not have had the courage to suggest this, were it not that my search program turned up an Ohr HaChaim HaKadosh to BeMidbar 14:22 which makes precisely this claim. Apparently, the use of *koli,* even in an entirely unconnected context, is naturally thought to refer to *Aseres HaDibros*. Certainly, then, in the very *parshah* in which *Aseres HaDibros* are central, it is reasonable to assume that *koli* would be automatically understood to refer to them.

So it turns out that the Ribono shel Olam made two conditions before He would trust us with His Torah. We must undertake to accept that which God will demand of us in *Aseres HaDibros,* and we must be true to the *bris* that the Ribono shel Olam had made with Avraham.

I believe that this is what Ramban had in mind when, in his comment in VaEira, he mentioned the fact that the Ribono shel Olam would become the God of our nation to all eternity when we will have accepted the Torah at Sinai. As we have worked out the meaning of the Yisro passage, "Torah" in this context would mean *Aseres HaDibros*.[3]

There is much work ahead of us, but before we move on, we should sum up what we have accomplished up to now. Let us look once more at the crucial verse that we have been discussing:

> ועתה אם שמוע תשמעו בקלי ושמרתם את בריתי והייתם לי סגלה מכל העמים . . .

> Now, if you listen carefully to My voice and will be true to My covenant, you shall become My very own possession [chosen] from among all the nations [although] the whole earth is Mine [and I could have chosen any of them.]

When Israel arrived in the Sinai desert, the very first thing that the Ribono shel Olam conveyed to them in anticipation of *Ma'amad Har Sinai* was a promise wrapped in some conditions. They were about to become His "very own possession," chosen from among all the nations of the world. However, two conditions were attached. As we have worked it out, the first one was that they would undertake to abide by the demands made in *Aseres HaDibros.* The second condition was that they were to conscientiously live with the awareness that this state of existence as a chosen people was built into Jewish destiny from the very beginning of their history. It was to be the fulfillment of the *bris* that the Ribono shel Olam had concluded with Avraham.

Since these two conditions are mentioned together, it seems to me that they must be connected with each other. We shall explore that relationship in the coming chapter.

Come! There is much that we can discover together.

FOUR

The Luchos *as "Testimonial" and as "Covenant"*

We ended the previous chapter having recognized that the two conditions that the Ribono shel Olam laid down for accepting us as His *segulah* were interconnected. You will recall that, according to the Ramban whom we are going to follow in these essays, these conditions were that: a. we would obey the obligations laid down in the *Aseres HaDibros,* and b. we would remain loyal to, and recognize ourselves bound by, the *bris* that the Ribono shel Olam had forged with Avraham Avinu. It established that we and all our descendants would live to all eternity as a people under God.

☞ THE FOLLOWING PARAGRAPH SHOULD BE READ VERY CAREFULLY. IT ENCAPSULATES THE ESSENCE OF THE ENTIRE BOOK.

That interconnectedness can be expressed as follows: The family of Avraham enjoys a unique relationship with the Ribono shel Olam. That relationship is, so to speak, three-legged. We are the Ribono shel Olam's *segulah,* and, presumably as a consequence, are to carry ourselves as a *Mamleches Kohanim* and a *Goy Kadosh.* These descriptions have teeth. They are not simply a series of compliments, but shoulder us with onerous duties. They require us to live these qualities in real time. But how? How are we to know how a *Mamleches Kohanim* and a *Goy Kadosh* act? The *Dibros* are the answer. They codify the *constitutional principles* upon which the national and religious life of a community defined by these terms is to unfold. The significance of these *Dibros* lies not in their binding nature as *mitzvos*—although most[1] or all of them do indeed have *mitzvah* status—but in the fact that each of them demands one particular form of behavior, one cluster of attitudes that forms the irreducible essence of a people charged with a destiny such as ours.[2]

The present chapter will be devoted to the challenging task of demonstrating that this is indeed the case.

Our first step must be to reiterate and make absolutely clear that "*Dibra*"[3] is not synonymous with "*mitzvah.*" *Aseres*

HaDibros are *not* Ten Commandments. Rambam, in his Sefer HaMitzvos, finds altogether fourteen *mitzvos*[4] within *Aseres HaDibros*. So, of what are there ten? There are ten *Dibros* although there are fourteen *mitzvos*.

What, then, is a *Dibra*? We said earlier that each of them lays down a form of behavior and a set of attitudes, which, collectively, define the peoplehood of Klal Yisrael. We will now take this a little further.

Aseres HaDibros are of course inseparable from the *luchos*, the tablets into which they were engraved. If we can discover a little more about the nature of these tablets, we might be able to form a more solid opinion about *Aseres HaDibros* themselves.

The Torah has some interesting expressions when speaking of the *luchos*. In Shemos 31:18, 32:15, and 34:29 they are called *Luchos HaEidus*, the tablets that bear testimony, and in Devarim 9:9, 9:11, and 9:15 we have them called *Luchos HaBris*, the tablets that bear the covenant. Now, since blank stone tablets are neither *testimony* nor *covenant*, it follows that these terms refer to the text that was engraved upon them. *Aseres HaDibros* themselves are both testimony and covenant.

Indeed, both usages appear unselfconsciously in the Torah even when they are not modifiers of *luchos*. For example, Shemos 40:20 speaks of Moshe Rabbeinu placing the *eidus* in the ark. Rashi remarks that this refers to the *luchos*. Now clearly the "*eidus*" status of the *luchos* derived from what was engraved upon them. It is the *Dibros* that are the real *testimony*.[5] Together with this source we should also list the many times that the ark, the *aron*, is called *Aron HaEidus* (Shemos 25:22 is the first time), and the Mishkan is called *Mishkan HaEidus* (Shemos 38:21 is the first time). Both expressions clearly derive from the fact that the *luchos*, read *Aseres HaDibros*, are lying in the ark, which is placed in the Mishkan. So we conclude that *Aseres HaDibros* are a "testimonial."

For *bris* we have Shemos 34:28, which speaks of "*Divrei HaBris, Aseres HaDevarim*," the words of the *bris* that ARE *Aseres HaDevarim*. Clearly the *Dibros* are themselves the *bris*. And we often have the expression *Aron Bris HaShem*, the ark [containing] the *bris* of HaShem (BeMidbar 10:33 is the first time). The ark is "the ark of the covenant of HaShem" because it contains the *luchos* upon which *Aseres HaDibros* are engraved.[6]

So *Aseres HaDibros* are a combination of "*eidus*" and "*bris*," a testimony and a covenant.

But to what do they testify (*eidus*)? What covenant (*bris*) do they express? I cannot understand why, as far as I have been able to discover, neither Rashi nor Ramban addresses this question. Now, I have found one place where Ramban quotes a Chazal that might help. See his comments to Devarim 9:17 where he offers explanations why, in the particular context in which it occurs, Moshe Rabbeinu found it necessary to mention that he had broken the tablets:

> ויתכן שירמוז עוד לטובה שעשה עמהם, כי סכן בנפשו לשבור לוחות האלהים לטובתם, כאשר אמרו רבותינו (שמו"ר מג א) מוטב תדון בפנויה ולא באשת איש.
>
> It is moreover possible that Moshe Rabbeinu was hinting at a favor that he had done the Israelites. He had risked his life for their sakes by breaking the tablets. It was to their benefit that the tablets were broken, as Chazal teach at Shemos Rabba 43:1. They compare Israel at that time to a woman who has illicit relationships at a time when she is about to get married. It is much better that she should be judged as an unmarried woman than that she be judged as a married woman.

Apparently, the tablets were to be considered as the equivalent of the marriage ring.[7] They were symbolic of a union between Klal Yisrael and the Ribono shel Olam. Had they served the *eigel* after they had already received the *luchos,* there could have been no forgiveness.

Now, Malachi 2:14 speaks of a wife as an *eishes brisechah,* a woman with whom you have forged a covenant. When we speak of the tablets as *luchos ha'eidus,* or *luchos habris,* we mean that they are the symbolism of an intimate relationship between the Ribono shel Olam and ourselves.

Accordingly, we may say that at this point we have achieved a clear and satisfying sense of what happened on the second of Sivan, the day after Benei Yisrael arrived at Midbar Sin. That day, as Ramban appears to understand it, was devoted to what we might call some housekeeping that had to be attended to before *Matan Torah* could take place. It was the day upon which the *bris* that the Ribono shel Olam had forged with Avraham Avinu was to be brought to the threshold of actualization. The Jews were told that they had it in their power to achieve a *segulah* status vis-à-vis the Ribono shel Olam if they would be willing to abide by the covenant that the Ribono shel Olam had made with Avraham. The actual consummation would take place a few days later. They would receive *Aseres HaDibros,* which, when they will have been inscribed upon the *luchos* and handed to them, would, so to speak, be the wedding ring with which the Ribono shel Olam would make them His own.

This spells out the interconnectedness between the two conditions that were laid down in verse 5. We are adjured to be heedful of the *kol* (read *Aseres HaDibros*), because it is they who give body to the relationship that bound Avraham Avinu and his family (now defined as *Mamleches Kohanim VeGoy Kadosh*) to the Ribono shel Olam for all eternity.

This moves us forward quite a bit, but we are not yet home free. We still need to ask ourselves why just these fourteen *mitzvos,* dressed up as ten *Dibros,* are the constituent parts of this *eidus* or *bris*. Why does the prohibition against giving false testimony (*Dibur* 9) make the cut, but, let us say in a purely arbitrary selection, the prohibition against oppressing widows and orphans (Shemos 22:21) does not? Why the insistence, in this context, that we not covet our friend's possessions (*Dibur* 10), but an apparent disregard for the evils of taking vengeance or bearing a grudge (VaYikra 19:18)?

These questions are going to be hard to answer. The issues are, after all, not anything that can be pinned down with any certainty. Nevertheless, I will try to make some suggestions in the coming chapters.[8]

Come, we have much to do.

FIVE

Rashi on K'sheih Oref

This chapter marks a turning point in our book. The first four chapters were required to establish what, in Ramban's view, was really happening at *Ma'amad Har Sinai*. From now on we will be able to deal with the implications. We will be able to ask—and to some extent, with appropriate care and awareness of our limitations, to answer—some very important questions. What does participation in these unique experiences say about us in our relationship with the Ribono shel Olam? What does this relationship demand of us? Who are we? What is a good and reasonable definition of our tasks in life? Yes, there is a lot that we must do. Let us pray to the Ribono shel Olam that we will turn in a creditable job.

Let us set the ball rolling by asking an apparently simple question that will, in the following essay, yield an extremely profound answer. Here is the question. What does the Ribono shel Olam most want that we should know concerning His relationship with us? What mistaken idea does He most of all want us to avoid? What, in short, is the defining element of Jewishness? I believe that this is a good question to ask, because the answer will be more than an answer. It will be a key to the understanding of much else in Judaism about which it is important that we be clear.

Let us approach our subject obliquely. We will get where we need to get in good time. In this case this means the next chapter.

We need to take a fresh look at the story of the *Eigel*. The following verses are the ones that concern us here.

ז. וידבר יהוה אל משה לך רד כי שחת עמך אשר העלית מארץ מצרים.
ח. סרו מהר מן הדרך אשר צויתם עשו להם עגל מסכה וישתחוו לו ויזבחו לו ויאמרו אלה אלהיך ישראל אשר העלוך מארץ מצרי.
ט. ויאמר יהוה אל משה ראיתי את העם הזה והנה עם קשה ערף הוא.

7. HaShem spoke to Moshe, "Go down, for the people whom you brought out of Egypt have become corrupt.
8. "They have been quick to leave the way that I ordered

them to follow, and they have made for themselves a cast-metal calf. They have bowed down to it and offered sacrifices to it, exclaiming, 'This, Israel is your god who brought you out of Egypt.'"
9. God the said to Moshe, "I have observed the people and they are a stubborn nation."[1]

Moshe Rabbeinu is up on Mount Sinai and the Ribono shel Olam has just given him the [first] *luchos*. Suddenly, everything comes crumbling down. Without warning the Ribono shel Olam moves in with His dreadful news. The people, who so recently had declared their unconditional loyalty to their God, had proved themselves fickle and apparently largely untouched by the Sinaitic experience. All hopes that a productive and fruitful relationship between them and their God might develop have been frustrated. There seems only one reasonable reaction to their treasonable behavior. God will simply rid Himself of this hapless mass of failures. He would start again from the beginning. The seed of the Avos had had their chance and had proved themselves too small for greatness. A new people would have to be picked. Moshe Rabbeinu and his family would be the ones to carry the burden and exhilaration of being God's chosen through history.[2] God's plans for mankind would remain what they had always been; the agency through which they would reach fulfillment would be changed.

Is this an accurate description of what happened? I think that it sounds reasonable enough and seems capable of explaining God's expressed intention, *And now, let go of Me and allow My anger to rage against them and I will destroy them and make you into a great nation* (Shemos 32:10). However, I think that what I have written is either completely wrong, or, if it contains any grains of truth, that truth seems certainly not to be yielded by the words that the Torah uses. For it is not at all what God said. What the Ribono shel Olam did say (there, verse 9) was something quite different. It was this: *I have observed this nation and it is a stiff-necked[3] one.*

Now what does *that* mean? How does the fact that they

made the *eigel* show that they are stiff-necked? Moreover, even if it were established that, in fact, they are an obstinate people, is that a reason to destroy them? Is not our love for the Ribono shel Olam a stiff-necked love? Let us recall the Mechilta that Ramban brings as an interpretation of *Those who love Me,* in Shemos 20:6:

—How come you are being dragged out to be killed?
—It is because I circumcised my son.
—How come you are being dragged out to be burned at the stake?
—It is because I was studying Torah.
—How come you are being dragged out to be crucified?
—It is because I ate matzah.
—How come you are being dragged out to be flogged by your jailer?
—It is because I held the *lulav.*

Thank God that we are indeed a stiff-necked people! Are we to be destroyed by the Ribono shel Olam because of that?

Rashi has this to say: "They turn their stiff neck toward those who point out their errors and refuse to listen." Apparently he means to say that Israel was to be destroyed, not because they were stiff-necked, but because of their sin in making and worshipping the *eigel.* Their obstinacy is relevant only because it precluded any expectation that they would ever be forgiven. For people who refuse to listen, the gates of repentance must forever remain closed. They were so obstinately wrongheaded that they were incapable of ever understanding how wrong they really were. No amount of *musar* would ever help, and therefore there would never be any change.

But is that true? Are we, as Jews, really incapable of admitting error? Ramban points out in his commentary (see Ramban Shemos 32:1) that all it took for the Jews to back down from their heresy was for Moshe to come down from the mountain. He burns the *eigel,* he grinds it down and forces the people to drink of the purifying waters, all without any objection from anyone. Later on, he engages the Ribono shel Olam in the epic battle for forgiveness, which results in the revelation of the thirteen attributes of mercy. The people *did* repent; they *were* forgiven. What, as Rashi appears to understand God's stricture, could He possibly have meant?[4]

Ramban, over here, is silent. It occurred to me that it is possible to work out a completely different approach for the Ramban, one that is consonant with ideas that he expresses on other occasions.

SIX

Ramban on K'sheih Oref

Here is the question with which we began the last chapter:

> What does the Ribono shel Olam most want that we should know concerning His relationship with us? What mistaken idea does He most of all want us to avoid?

As we were making our way toward a solution, we wondered why, when we made the *eigel,* it was our stubbornness[1] that most troubled the Ribono shel Olam. We saw how Rashi understood the term, but we were unable to decipher his meaning in that particular context.

As we have often done in this series of books, we turned to the Ramban to see whether he would offer us guidance. We found that Ramban made no comment on the phrase that we are trying to understand. That certainly did not help us directly, but I have the feeling that it does help us just a little bit.

Throughout his commentary on Chumash, Ramban is so generous, his largesse is so lavish, his intuitive understanding of our needs is so on the mark, that, though I have never heard this stated in so many words, I feel that we can say for him, as we say about Rashi, that his omissions must be viewed as commissions. If Ramban is silent it is only because all that is necessary has already been said.

Ramban trusted us to do our homework. Let us not fail him.

Let us take an inventory of what we already know. Clearly, so the Torah tells us, the *Cheit HaEigel* betrayed a lethal stubbornness—enough to persuade the Ribono shel Olam that He must wipe the slate clean and make a completely new beginning. The Ribono shel Olam did not say that this people whom He had delivered from Egypt were displaying a propensity toward idol worship or that they had a rebellious nature that drove them to do the opposite of what they were called upon to do. He did not blame them for being impetuous, for acting without due consideration, or for being vain in believing themselves to have the right to be arbiters of what the ideal form of worship might be. It was stubbornness and only stubbornness that weighed so heavily upon the scale of Jewish fate.

Why? And more to the point, what role did stubbornness play in the whole disaster? It seems to me that we can read the story, even read it carefully, without stumbling onto any part of it that suggests just that quality. Assuredly there was much that was blameworthy in what we did. But how were we stubborn?

Well, there is no possible way in which we can find that out, unless we know what precisely went wrong. What triggered the people's despair? What precisely did they mean to accomplish? In what way was a golden figure, produced only now from their own jewelry, going to be of any help to them?

Here is Ramban's suggestion.

> הנה משה נאבד ממנו. נעשה לנו משה אחר שיורה הדרך לפנינו על פי ה' בידו . . .
>
> אבל הענין כמו שאמרתי, שלא בקשו העגל להיות להם לאל ממית ומחיה, וקבלו עבודת אלהותו עליהם, אבל ירצו שיהיה להם במקום משה מורה דרכם.
>
> [They certainly were not asking for another God] but requested only another "Moshe." They argued,] "Moshe who led us from the time we left Egypt until now . . . is no longer with us. Let us then make another "Moshe" who, inspired by God, will lead us on the right road. . . ." They never thought of the *eigel* as a God with life and death in its hands, or that they should serve it as one would serve a God. All they wanted was someone who could replace Moshe, to guide them along the road they would have to travel.[2]

They were certainly wrong, but withal, it sounds like an innocent enough idea. Indeed, Ramban goes on to explain how

Aaron used this very interpretation of what happened to mitigate the blame of his own complicity.

And yet, God was willing to destroy them for what they had done, or better, for the obstinacy that they had displayed in doing it. He was willing to erase from His memory Avraham's love, Yitzchak's self-sacrifice, Yaakov's integrity. The epic struggles to establish monotheism, the kindness and the caring, the battles and the victories, Israel's loyalty through two centuries of abject slavery. Sarah's wisdom, Rivkah's kindness, Leah's determination to win her husband's love, Rachel's self-sacrifice for her sister—and how she would weep, standing by her lonely grave, when millions of her children would have been consigned to millions of equally lonely, useless, unvisited graves—all, all would land up on the slag heap of history. It would all turn out to have been so much wasted energy. What had been built with such loving hands would lie in ruins. What God had nurtured with so much patience would be no more.

It seems to have been a small enough mistake. Could there really be no forgiveness?

No! Without Moshe Rabbeinu's intercession, there could not. They were a stiff-necked people and for such, the gates of mercy had been slammed shut.[3]

How are we to understand all this?

Our first stop will once again be the Ramban, but this time not at his Chumash commentary but in his essay, Toras HaShem Temimah.[4] In that essay he makes the following statement: *It is clear that they thought that Moshe Rabbeinu acted as an intermediary between them and God and he had now left them. Accordingly they asked Aaron [to make something that could replace Moshe.]*

Apparently the idea that we would require an intermediary between ourselves and the Ribono shel Olam is particularly shocking. Why?

There is a small passage in *parashas* Yisro that is hard to understand. Here is why. The drama of *Matan Torah* is told toward the end of the *parshah*; it runs from Shemos 19:1 till

20:13. From 20:14 till 20:17 there is a short interlude in which Moshe Rabbeinu assuages the people's fears concerning the shattering experience that they had just lived through. We could really say that those few *pesukim* are still a part of the *Ma'amad Har Sinai* narrative. After that there are five more *pesukim* and with those Yisro comes to a close. Immediately after that, *parshas* Mishpatim begins. Our interest is in those five *pesukim*. They list a number of *mitzvos* and we are hard put to understand why that list, made up of those particular *mitzvos*, belongs here. They seem to be just hanging there without a compelling relationship to either what came before them or what was to follow.

Our challenge is to explain the logic of having this passage here, immediately following upon the story of *Aseres HaDibros*.

In order not to stray too far afield, we will cite only the first of this series of *pesukim*, together with Ramban's explanation. The nature of the issues involved will require me to marshal a number of different Rambans. The information that we will require is not all to be found in one place. I will cite the various sources as we draw on them.

Here is another piece of information before we get started on this section. You will note that the translation that I offer for the following two verses does not comply with the *trope*. Nor is the translation literal. Ramban, for reasons sufficiently compelling for him, was apparently willing to live with these problems. For us it is sufficient to note that they exist.

Here we go.

יט. ויאמר יהוה אל משה כה תאמר אל בני ישראל אתם ראיתם כי מן השמים דברתי עמכם.

כ. לא תעשון אתי אלהי כסף ואלהי זהב לא תעשו לכם.

19. HaShem spoke to Moshe, "So shall you say to the Israelites, 'You have witnessed that I spoke to you from the heavens.

20. Do not believe that there might be gods of silver and gold together with Me. Moreover [even without entertaining such a belief] do not even make them!' "

We will begin by asking how verse 20 follows logically on verse 19. Here is what Ramban (Shemos 20:19) writes:

> From the fact that I spoke to you from the heavens it will be obvious to you that I am Master of both the heavens and the earth. Therefore do not think that you will gain any advantage by partnering Me with any "god" made of silver or gold. It should be clear to you that you have no need for anybody who is together with Me and might be of help to you.

Ramban has opened up two propositions that we ought to consider. The first, that people might have supposed that having some additional "gods" might be an advantage to them; the second, that the Ribono shel Olam's unchallenged control of heaven and earth obviates any such supposed gain.

What advantage might the people have anticipated? For that we can turn to Ramban to Devarim 22:19. That verse proclaims, *Whoever sacrifices to any deity other than God alone must be condemned to death.*[5] He explains: The Torah writes this because the people who sacrificed to the angels thought that they were doing the right thing. They imagined that by doing so they were really acting in accordance with God's will. They assumed that the function of the angels was to act as intermediaries to elicit goodwill from Him and that therefore a sacrifice brought to them was really a sacrifice brought to God *together* with His servants. It is for that reason that the Torah writes, . . . *other than God* ALONE. There need not be, and therefore there may not be, any combination of the Ribono shel Olam with anybody else.

Let us absorb carefully what we have now learned. The *Aseres HaDibros* have been pronounced. One would have supposed that after that shattering experience there would be some kind of break to give the people time to accommodate themselves to all that had happened. But that was not to be. Immediately,[6] the Ribono shel Olam found it necessary to have Moshe Rabbeinu teach the people that they would never require any kind of intermediary between themselves and the Ribono shel Olam.

Why could this not have waited? Why was it so urgent that they should know just this *mitzvah* without any delay at all?

Evidently, it was so important because it is the answer to the question that we posed in the previous chapter and repeated at the beginning of this one. We have now discovered what it is about our Judaism that the Ribono shel Olam most wants us to know. It is this matter of immediate and unmediated access to Him. Nothing in Judaism is more important than that. That is the second proposition offered by the Ramban and it is that which I would now like to explore further.

I would like to understand the theory. The Ribono shel Olam is our king. That is a lesson that we learned very clearly at Sinai. But is it a necessary function of kingship that each of his subjects should have immediate and unmediated access to him?[7] I would have supposed that the rule that a king is not able to forgo the honor that is his due[8] would, to the contrary, demand a measure of restraint.

I suspect that the answer must be that, if the Ribono shel Olam were *only* our king, if there were no other way in which He related to us, then indeed things might have been different. Of course the Ribono shel Olam is our King, but He is also very much besides.

Let us take Yechezkel 34 where the Ribono shel Olam is depicted as the compassionate shepherd of His flock as an example. No task is demeaning; no need, great or small, too insignificant. Where Yehudah's kings had failed because they acted like kings and not like shepherds, the Ribono shel Olam would succeed. A king is indeed not permitted to forgo the honor that is due to him, but that is true only as long as it is the "king" character that preponderates at a given moment. Shed the kingship and don the shepherd's crook, as dictated by the circumstances, and everything changes radically.[9]

Perhaps there is no passage in our literature that describes the real relationship that the Ribono shel Olam wants to have with us as vividly as does Ibn Gabirol in his "Keser Malchus":

Ramban on K'sheih Oref

לכן אם תקטלני לך איחל
ואם תבקש לעוני, אברח ממך אליך
ואתכסה מחמתך בצלך.
ובשולי רחמיך אחזיק
עד אם רחמתני
ולא אשלחך כי אם ברכתני.

Therefore were You to kill me—
I would yet place my hope in You
Were You eager to find out my sins I would flee
from You—to You
I would seek shelter from Your anger—in Your Shadow
I would hold tight upon the hems of your garment of mercy—
Until You had showered me with mercy.
I would not let You go—
until You had showered Your blessings upon me.

Those immortal words, *to flee from You—to You,* are the ones to remember and carry—or let them carry us—through life. They make the thought that maybe some form of a go-between might be useful seem ridiculous.

Really, we always realized this. After the sea had split seven weeks earlier, Israel had sung, *This is my God and I will make an abode for Him* (Targum to Shemos 15:2).[10] God would, so to speak, be our next-door neighbor. You do not send an ambassador to borrow a cup of sugar.

From the very first moment when we arrived at Sinai, it seems that the Ribono shel Olam had been concerned that we understand exactly the kind of relationship that He wished to forge with the children of the Avos who had served Him so loyally. The very first words that He spoke to us through Moshe Rabbeinu had been redolent with love and caring: "Remember how you witnessed the unleashing of My fury against your oppressors!"[11] "Remember the eagle's wings that brought you here; the impatience with which I awaited your coming!" Where He might have ordered, He persuaded; the mode was one of love and caring rather than of authority.[12] He had promised that we were to become His *segulah,* the precious possession from which He would never be able to bring Himself to part. He was going to make very sure that, from the first moment the feeling of living in the Ribono shel Olam's embrace would be the reality within which we would be nurtured.

And what can, what must, be said of us? We were deaf to the implications. Stubbornly, we insisted on judging the relationship that the Ribono shel Olam was proposing, in the old terms with which we were familiar. "Kings" we understood. We had experienced centuries under Pharaoh. That authority itself could eschew power and express itself in love was a concept that was beyond us. Where the Ribono shel Olam saw Himself as a Chasan, we were incapable of seeing ourselves as a bride. "Let God Himself speak to us. We wish to hear our orders from the king Himself, not from His chamberlain. We wish to see our king!" (Rashi, Shemos 19:9). This, even after all that had happened, was as much as we could manage. And when the real test came, we failed dismally. Moshe Rabbeinu seems to have disappeared and our very first thought was of the need to fashion a go-between. We were indeed a stiff-necked people, unable to tear ourselves away from our preconceived notions of what form this new, unique relationship would take. We traded our glory, the close intimacy that God had offered us, for a *grass-munching ox* (Tehilim 106:20). It is a sad story, is it not? We can begin to understand the Ribono shel Olam's wish to make a fresh beginning.

In the coming chapter we will get a glimpse of just how glorious that new relationship was planned to be.

SEVEN

Matan Torah—*God's Wedding Day*

This was one Chasunah that we would not have wanted to miss. Apart from everything else, we were the Kallah.[1]

Let us begin by quoting from Mishnayos Ta'anis 4:8. We will be touching on issues that we already discussed in the previous chapter. They can use some fleshing out.

Here is the Mishnah:

> וכן הוא אומר, (שיר השירים ג) צאינה וראינה בנות ציון במלך שלמה בעטרה שעטרה לו אמו ביום חתנתו וביום שמחת לבו. ביום חתנתו, זו מתן תורה. וביום שמחת לבו, זה בנין בית המקדש, שיבנה במהרה בימינו. אמן.
>
> . . . And thus too does it say *O Zion's daughters, go out so that you may see King Shlomo wearing the crown that his people*[2] *made for him to wear on the day of his wedding, the day of his joy.* "The day of his wedding," that refers to the day of *Matan Torah.*[3] "The day of his joy," that refers to the building of Beis HaMikdash.

The day of *Matan Torah* is the day upon which the Ribono shel Olam found His *zivug.* Everything flows from that; it is the underlying theme that, in the end, will make everything clear. We, who are struggling to find out what is going on, are like first-time guests at a Jewish wedding. We know that all the strange bits and pieces must have some valid role to play, but we are missing the tools to put it all together. We need a guide to untangle things for us. We are blessed to have the late, great R. Shimshon Pincus זצ"ל take us by the hand, allowing us a peek into a world of which he was a denizen but of which most of us know very little. We will loosely paraphrase a few excerpts from his peerless essay, *BePischei She'arim,* the introduction to his Tif'eres Torah.[4]

He begins by pointing out how vital it is that, whatever the undertaking in which we may be engaged, we never lose sight of what precisely is the purpose of that venture. It is always possible and forgivable to forget this or that detail that is important to the success of the project, but it is forbidden to forget what the project is all about. For example, we might agree that the essential nature of a business is to provide an income for the owner. So if I open a supermarket, I may make some silly mistakes in pricing my offerings. I may, for example, forget that Yom Tov is around the corner and that, for the next couple of weeks, there will be a tremendous surge in demand. That is forgivable. But if I forget that the entire purpose of the market is to help me make a living, and instead act as though the store is there to provide attractive displays of vegetables for my neighbors' esthetic edification, then I am not a grocer but a fool.

From there, R. Pincus moves to the institution of marriage. There are certainly aspects to a marriage that deal with the mechanics of daily living. Who goes to work and who does the cooking? Who cleans the house and who shovels the snow? Who drives the carpools and who supervises the homework? These are legitimate questions and the details that they involve must be worked out. However, if someone were to define marriage as no more than a contract within which the flotsam and jetsam of housekeeping chores are equitably distributed, he would obviously be hopelessly at sea. Marriage is the intimacy between husband and wife, the mutual feelings of closeness and respect, the determination to become partners, energized as if by one heart and one soul, in building a home or, better, in building a "life together." Marriage as it truly plays itself out is, or should be, a matter of an exquisite understanding and empathy between husband and wife. It is a story to which dry cleaners and snow tires have nothing to add.

It is in this sense that we are called upon to understand the *bris* of *Ma'amad Har Sinai,* once Chazal have taught us that *Matan Torah* is *the day of His wedding.* It is the creation of a relationship of love and caring, of cleaving and intimacy. When brought to actualization at its fullest potential it has in its power the ability to change every aspect of our lives. It is an utterly transforming concept.

Here is a translation of a section in R. Pincus's essay.

Let us go back to the *pasuk* that begins with the words *You have witnessed what I have done to Egypt.* I truly believe that the following is the simple, straightforward meaning of the verse. In the marital covenant the most fundamental need of a wife is to know that she means something to her husband, that he cares about her.[5] She fears that she may be of no importance to him. It is for this reason that the Ribono shel Olam said, "The whole world is Mine. Many tragedies unfortunately occur . . . but, for all that, there are limits. No destruction is ever total. Has it ever happened that all the waters of a country turned to blood? Come what may, water always remains water. Egypt was different. All the water turned into blood. Have you ever heard of a country overrun by frogs? Croaking in the ovens? Rumbling in people's stomachs? Or have you ever heard of a plague of lice as this one was?" The Ribono shel Olam tells us, "Have I ever treated another country thus? That all its dust turned into lice? Have you ever heard of wild animals overrunning an inhabited land? Don't you see that whatever I brought upon Egypt lay completely outside the boundaries erected by the normalcy of nature?

"Plainly and simply, the Egyptians drove me to act as I would never act under normal circumstances.[6] How did they do it? Why did I react as I did? Because they mistreated you—and I cared, cared profoundly and desperately about you. One who touches you touches, as it were, the apple of the divine eye."

This is the opening salvo in the drama of *Ma'amad Har Sinai*. "You can see how much you matter to Me. Think of a father, a quiet, decent, person who suddenly acts completely out of character when somebody hurts his only child. We might even say that, in his fury, he acts inappropriately. But that is what "caring" does to him. Look how much your pain hurt Me. See how much I care. If one could use the word when referring to the Ribono shel Olam we would say, "They drove Me 'crazy'!"[7]

These are the first words that the Ribono shel Olam

> spoke to us when we came to Sinai. "Never say that I do not care! I care. Oh, how much I care! I care deeply and suffer for My caring." This is the ABC of Judaism. Without this knowledge, nothing even begins.[8]

Interestingly enough, just as the opening phrase of *Ma'amad Har Sinai* begins with the words, YOU HAVE SEEN *what I did to Mitzrayim . . . ,* so too does the verse immediately following *Ma'amad Har Sinai* begin with those selfsame words: YOU HAVE SEEN *that I spoke to you from the heavens. . . . Aseres HaDibros* are bracketed by these two phrases. It is as though the Ribono shel Olam is urging us to take Him seriously. "Your own senses," He is saying to us. "Your own senses testify to the sheer rightness of what I am offering you. You witnessed that I put My own integrity and My own honor on the line. I punished the Egyptians more than would normally have seemed reasonable. I have spoken to you from the very heavens disregarding your very human fallibility. What more should it take to convince you that this is the perfect *shiduch* for you?!"

That understood, we must still dredge this *pasuk* for all the meaning that is hidden in it. Unfortunately, this time we do not have Rav Pincus's thoughts to inspire us. Still we can make a guess at what he might have said, by looking further at some of his thoughts on marriage.

In the course of his argument that marriage is infinitely more than simply the sum of the various obligations that husband and wife undertake toward each other, R. Pincus broaches another topic. He asks, rhetorically of course, why the Kesubah document that lists the husband's obligations toward his wife does not stipulate that he is obliged to communicate with her, to speak to her, to have conversations with her. His answer is that communication lies at the very crux of marriage. It is not a contractual obligation but the stuff of which the relationship itself is made. Where there is no intimate communication there is no marriage. If a husband does not speak to his wife, nor she to him, they remain strangers to each other even if they both conscientiously perform all the obligations that the contract imposes upon them.

Now, Rashi and Ramban both deal with the apparent contradiction between the statements that the Ribono shel Olam "came down" onto Mount Sinai (Shemos 19:20) and His own assertion that He spoke to us from the heavens (20:19). They argue about certain details, but essentially agree that the Ribono shel Olam Himself remained in the heavens but that some aspect of His being descended upon the mountain.

Taking all this together, I suspect that we are well on our way to understanding the verse at Shemos 20:19 more profoundly than we did up to now.

It occurs to me that the following is probably the correct way of reading this text. Let us for a moment give some thought to what is not said in this verse rather than on what is. It does not say, "You have witnessed that I came down upon the mountain," but, "You have witnessed that I spoke to you from the heavens." Why? It seems to me that we must read the verse as follows: "You have witnessed that [although an aspect of My glory had descended upon the mountain and I could presumably have communicated with you through that aspect, I did not do so. Had I done so, our communication would have taken place through an intermediary since 'I' remained in the heavens, and relative to that 'I,' that aspect of My glory that descended upon the mountain, would have had the character of an intermediary.] I spoke to you from the heavens [insisting upon direct communication, because that is the only acceptable form of communication in the new 'marital' relationship that I am about to forge with you.]"

We can readily see that from this introduction the next verse, the one that we examined in the previous chapter, flows very smoothly. There is clearly no reason why we should ever feel the need to create images of gold or silver to act as intermediaries between us and the Ribono shel Olam. At *Ma'amad Har Sinai,* the Ribono shel Olam's "wedding day" to Klal Yisrael, His ecstatic bride established a relationship with Him that makes all artificialities false. From that day onward, the Ribono shel Olam's door remained constantly open to us. Deny that, and you have become a *min,* a heretic, as surely as you would have earned that title of opprobrium had you denied the Ribono shel Olam Himself (Rambam, Hilchos Teshuvah 3:7).

In chapter 9 we will begin our analysis of the individual *Dibros* that together constitute *Aseres HaDibros*. We will be trying to establish whether we are justified in viewing each one of them as a "constitutional principle" of a *Mamleches Kohanim VeGoy Kadosh*. However, before we get there, chapter 8 will attempt to pin down some ideas about *Aseres HaDibros* as a group. That is an important introduction to our examination of the individual *Dibros*. Come, we have much to learn.

EIGHT

Aseres Hadibros

Before we begin our analysis of the individual *Dibros*[1] in the next chapter, we should have one final summing up of what we already know. In this chapter you will not find very much that is new, but a little reviewing of ideas already absorbed never hurt anyone. It is a short chapter and should prove to be relatively painless. We will present our review in the form of answers to questions that anyone would reasonably ask.

Let us start with the following:

> What *are Aseres HaDibros*? Are they simply *mitzvos* or are they something more? If they are simply *mitzvos*, why did just these *mitzvos* have to be given with so much pomp when all the others were simply conveyed to Moshe Rabbeinu by the Ribono shel Olam, after which Moshe passed them on to us in the Beis HaMidrash where Torah learning really belongs? If they are something more than simply *mitzvos*, what are they?

We already know the answers to these. Starting from chapter 4 the concept of *Aseres HaDibros* as constitutional principles that define the ethos of a *Mamleches Kohanim VeGoy Kadosh* has been our constant companion. However, for the sake of those of you who prefer their theories to have solid textual grounding, I will just sum up some of the considerations that have to come into play.

I suppose that the place to begin is to translate *Dibros* correctly. The noun *davar* can be used for *word*[2] or *matter*[3] and their synonyms. *Aseres HaDibros* are couched in words, but these cannot be meant by *Dibros*, since clearly there are more than ten. So we are down to "matters" which is a very neutral term and does not tell us much. I suppose that *mitzvos* could be called "matters," but *mitzvos* cannot be the subject since, as Rambam counts them, there are altogether fourteen *mitzvos* included in *Aseres HaDibros* while Ramban counts eleven.[4]

So the "*Dibros*" are neither "word" nor "*mitzvah*." What then are they? Of what are there ten?

Before we answer by giving a definition, we need to know how to identify a *Dibra*. How do we set about finding ten units, no more and no less, in the text? Perhaps we could use the assigned *trope*.[5] Throughout the Torah these cantillation marks serve as a kind of punctuation and might usefully be studied here. In contrast to the rest of the Torah for which the Mesorah provides a single *trope* system, for *Aseres HaDibros* there are two. They are known respectively as *Ta'am Elyon*, the exalted cantillation system, and *Ta'am Tachton*, the lower, or more ordinary system. In general terms[6] it may be stated that the *Ta'am Tachton* divides the text into sentences (*pesukim*) while the *Ta'am Elyon* divides it into *Dibros*.[7, 8]

Even those of you who generally do not bother with the Notes section might want to check out notes 6, 7, and 8, to find out just how problematic the seemingly simple matter of identifying ten discrete *Dibros* from the text can be. If the *Ta'am Elyon* would be the sole arbiter, there would be only nine, since *Ta'am Elyon* joins what we consider to be the first two *Dibros* into one. If instead we were to consider the division into *parshiyos* to be decisive, we would indeed end up with ten *Dibros*, but they would not be the same ten that are familiar to us. In the *parshah* division, what we consider the first two *Dibros* are combined into one, while the tenth *Dibra*, *Lo Tachmod*, is divided into two.

So, for identification of how the text of *Aseres HaDibros* yields ten discrete *Dibros*, we have no alternative to basing ourselves upon the *Mesorah*. The text, standing alone, cannot help us.

Once we know *which* the ten *Dibros* are, we need to know *what* a *Dibra* is. Of what are there ten? As I mentioned earlier, since chapter 4 we already know the answer: a *Dibra* is one of a group of ten that, together, define the ethos of a *Mamleches Kohanim VeGoy Kadosh*. Of course we cannot just leave it at that. We will need to work out exactly what message it is that each of these ten "matters" sends us[9] and why those messages are so vital to us who have undertaken to be the *Benei Bris* of the Ribono shel Olam. We shall begin this gigantic task in the next chapter and it will keep us busy through chapter 19.

What will we be looking for? We will be groping to uncover what the constituent parts of this ethos are. In the meantime we can say the following in very general terms.

Do you wish to know who and what a Jew is? Find someone who, consistently and thoughtfully, lives by these ten principles and you will meet a person who, among many other things, eats kosher, dances on Simchas Torah, puts his right shoe on before his left shoe but ties the left one first; who loves the Ribono shel Olam and stands in awe of Him, who eschews sha'atnez, shellfish, and ill-gotten gains, who does not bear grudges, and who shakes a *Lulav*. In short, you will make the acquaintance of an *ehrlicher Yid*. Welcome to the land of *amchah*! It is a beautiful place.

Clearly we will understand all this better after we will have studied the next eleven chapters that take each *Dibra* separately.

Before we finish, there is one more question that we ought to consider. It is this:

> Why was God's purpose in giving us these ten *Dibros* served best by His being present on the mountain?

We can answer this question on two levels. Here is the simpler one: it is because a Chasan wants to be present at His own Chasunah. This was the day when Israel would, so to speak, become His bride. It was the day for which He had created the world (see Rashi to Bereishis 1:31). He wanted to be there. He "needed" to be there.[10] And, above all, His Kallah needed Him to be there.

For the next and deeper level, I would recommend that you look once more at the second half of the rather lengthy Preface at the beginning of this book. What the metaphors "Chasan" and "Kallah" stand for is the joyful union between the Ribono shel Olam and ourselves. Let us remember that

Ma'amad Har Sinai took place on Shabbos and, while we are on the subject, let us remember what Shabbos really ought to look like.

> You are One and Your name is One and who is like Your people Israel, one nation on earth. The splendor of greatness and the crown of salvation, the day of contentment and holiness have You given to Your people. Avraham would rejoice, Yitzchak would exult, Yaakov and his children would rest on it. It is to be a rest of love and magnanimity, a rest of truth and faith, a rest of peace, serenity, tranquility, and security. A perfect rest in which You find favor. May Your children recognize and know that from You comes their rest and through their rest they will sanctify Your name.[11]

To be a *passige Shiduch*[12] for the Ribono shel Olam, we had to go through a transformation. We had to be *kashered,* so to speak, by the heavenly fire that engulfed the mountain. That fire comes only together with the Ribono shel Olam's presence.

We are now ready to start off on our examination of each of *Aseres HaDibros.*

NINE

The First Dibra

In the previous chapters, particularly in the last one, we have argued that the significance of *Aseres HaDibros* lies in the fact that they are the constitutional principles by which a *Mamleches Kohanim VeGoy Kadosh* that aspires to be a *segulah* to the Ribono shel Olam must be guided. Although each of these *Dibros* (with the possible exception of the first one) are also *mitzvos*, it is not their status as *mitzvos* that earned them their place upon the *luchos*. The truths to which these *luchos* testify (*luchos ha'eidus*), the covenant of which they are a symbol (*luchos habris*), lie outside the world of the dos and don'ts of commandments. They are meant to spell out, and to function as, the defining underpinnings of *yiddishkeit*.

In this and the following chapters it will be our task to examine each of the ten *Dibros* and to try our hand at identifying the underlying principles that may have earned it its place among the *Dibros*.

אנכי ה' אלהיך..., *I am HaShem your God...*

Rambam and Ramban agree that, in spite of the fact that this first *Dibra* is not worded as a commandment, it is still to be counted as one of the positive *mitzvos*.[1] Rambam (Sefer HaMitzvos, Positive Commands 1) defines the *mitzvah* that is articulated in this wording as *Ha'amonas HaElohus*,[2] which we will translate[3] as *belief in God*. Ramban (Glosses to Sefer HaMitzvos, Negative Commands 5) defines it as *Kabbalas Malchus Shamayim*, the obligation to accept God as king over us.[4, 5]

So much for the *mitzvah* aspect of this *pasuk*. What justifies its inclusion among the *Dibros*?

Of course we could just leave things as they are. Certainly belief in God and the obligation to declare Him king are in themselves sufficiently fundamental to Judaism to justify their inclusion. However, it seems to me that the fact that God introduces Himself as He Who took us out of Egypt broadens the implications. If all that were demanded would be that we are to believe in the Ribono shel Olam and to accept His kingship, there would be no need to mention that He brought us out of Egypt. Let us see if we can work out what "God as Redeemer" could be said to add to what we have already discovered.

We will get where we need to get by making a detour to the Torah's labor laws in VaYikra, chapter 25.

First, we will present a little bit of background.

An *eved Ivri* is a Jew who has been sold as a slave, either because utter destitution forced him to sell himself, or, if he stole and has no money to make restitution, Beis Din sold him so that he would be able to reimburse his victim.

In the relevant *parshiyos* the Torah stresses again and again that the *eved Ivri*'s spirit must not be broken. He cannot be sold in a slave market, or from the platform upon which slaves were normally made to stand; the transaction must be private and dignified. There are severe limits to the kind of service he can be expected to perform. Nothing in any way degrading of human dignity is permitted. Above all, he can never become the absolute chattel of his buyer. Whether he wants to or not, his servitude is to be terminated by the Yovel. Certainly there can be exigencies in any life that might call for a temporary retrenchment. But no Jew can ever barter away his essential freedom. In the year of universal freedom, he too must go free.

I have described some of the laws that govern the servitude of the *eved Ivri*. However, my presentation may well have produced a wrong impression. I seem to have put the need to safeguard human, or Jewish, dignity at the center of the Torah's considerations. That is true, but it is only partially true. In two *pesukim* the Torah invokes a different reason for these limitations. At Vayikra 25:42 we read, *For they are My servants*[6] *whom I took out of Egypt. They are not to be sold in the manner that slaves are sold.* Again, at Vayikra 25:52 we read as the reason for the fact that the *eved Ivri* must go free in the *Yovel* year, *For the Children of Israel are servants to Me; they are My servants whom I took out of Egypt.*

On both these *pesukim,* Rashi makes the same remark: *My contract precedes theirs.*[7] Clearly, Reuven's slave cannot sell himself to Shimon. The reason why, as Jews, we cannot sell ourselves, nor have Beis Din sell us into absolute slavery, is because, as a result of the fact that the Ribono shel Olam took us out of Mitzrayim, we became the absolute servants of the Ribono shel Olam. Nobody can "own" us, even we ourselves cannot own ourselves, because long before we came upon the scene, we were all indentured to the Ribono shel Olam. We cannot become absolute slaves to humans because we are—and have been since *Yetzi'as Mitzrayim*—absolute servants to the Ribono shel Olam.

I was right earlier when I expressed the idea that the laws of the *eved Ivri* derived from the need to protect human or Jewish dignity. However, in projecting the idea that that need was self-evident or, indeed, universal, I was not right. The dignity that stands at the center of these laws derives from our servitude to God. The servant of a king is himself equivalent to a king (Shavu'os 47b).[8]

> [Here is an interesting thought that I would like to share with you, although it has no direct bearing upon the argument that I am trying to develop. It seems to me that, from the Torah's wording, which denies the owner the right to force his slave to do demeaning work on the basis of the fact that God's contract predated his, it must logically follow that God *does* have the "right" to demand demeaning work from us. If our responsibilities to any human owner are limited only because of the Ribono shel Olam's prior rights, that implies that no limits ought to be placed upon what the Ribono shel Olam can demand of us.]

It turns out that when the Ribono shel Olam took us out of Mitzrayim, there were some very weighty consequences. Apparently, when we call Pesach *Zeman Cheiruseinu,* the season of our freedom, that description has to be qualified. In a "this-worldly" context we were in fact absolutely free. But, none of us can, nor would we want to, escape our "fourth dimension." In that aspect of our being, the part of us that really matters most, we once more became indentured. This time it was to the Ribono shel Olam.

And that leaves its mark. Many of us may not know it, but this servitude shackles us every morning and every evening as we stand in prayer before God.

Here is how. In Berachos 4b we learn that the *Amidah* has to follow hard upon *Kri'as Shema* with its *berachos* and that nothing should be permitted to interrupt the one from the other. The Gemara goes so far as to assert that whoever follows this ruling conscientiously is assured of a welcome in Olam HaBa.

The "Rabbeinu Yonah" commentary to the Rif in Berachos wonders why a *mitzvah* that is seemingly so simple to perform should have such far-reaching consequences. It is after all not such a difficult matter to refrain from talking at that point in our prayers. Here is the answer that the commentary proffers:

> שהטעם שזוכה לשכר גדול כזה מפני שהקב"ה כשגאלנו והוציאנו ממצרים היה להיותינו לו לעבדים, שנאמר, כי עבדי הם אשר הוצאתי אותם מארץ מצרים, ובברכת גאל ישראל מזכיר בה החסד שעשה עמנו הבורא. והתפלה היא עבודה . . . וכשהוא מזכיר יציאת מצרים ומתפלל מיד, מראה שכמו שהעבד שקנה אותו רבו חייב לעשות מצוות רבו, כן הוא מכיר הטובה והגאולה שגאל אותו הבורא ושהוא עבדו ועובד אותו. וכיון שמכיר שהוא עבדו מפני שגאלו ועושה רצונו ומצוותיו, נמצא שבעבור זה זוכה לחיי עולם הבא.

> The reason why adhering to this seemingly simple *mitzvah* guarantees such a huge reward is that God's intention in taking us out of Mitzrayim was that we should become His servants . . . Now in the final *berachah* of *Kri'as Shema* we mention the great kindness that the Ribono shel Olam did to us. Now prayer itself is a form of service.[9] Therefore if, immediately upon ending *Kri'as Shema,* he begins his prayer, he affirms that just as a slave who was bought by his master is obliged to do what the master demands of him, so he too recognizes the great favor that the Ribono shel Olam had done to him and the

good that He had bestowed upon him, and that therefore he has become His servant and must serve Him.

Once he has recognized his servant status and therefore commits himself to do His will and perform His commands, those actions—not the simple juxtaposition of the two sections in the Siddur—are what guarantees him a place in Olam HaBa.

It has become very clear that if we can bring ourselves to live Jewishly thoughtful lives, our entire day will be influenced by the truths conveyed to us in this *Dibra.* As we have defined the role of *Aseres HaDibros,* it has become abundantly clear that this first one—with its stress on *Yetzi'as Mitzrayim*—surely belongs among that select company.

TEN

The Second Dibra

לא יהיה לך אלהים אחרים על פני . . . , *Do not have any other gods before Me . . .*

How are we to view this *Dibra as* a *Dibra*? Where does it take us, beyond the actual prohibition against serving idols or making them, a prohibition that seems alien to us who have never experienced the dreadful urge to abnegate ourselves before a graven image?[1] Has it simply fallen into disuse? Have our *Aseres HaDibros,* for practical purposes, become nine?

Are you, dear Reader, ready for some really new ideas? Are you ready to absorb that this seemingly arcane *Dibra* is, in fact, more alive to us, more real for us, more demanding of us, than any of the other *Dibros*? Has it ever occurred to you that we might all be "idol worshippers," if not in the formal sense, then, at least, at heart—where things really count?

Let us explore some territory, where most of us have rarely been. We must brave the very predawn of our history. One of the words that appears constantly in the Torah's description of the six days of Creation is *lemino,* according to its kind.[2] As the Ribono shel Olam created the vegetable and animal worlds, He ordered that each species maintain its own characteristics and reproduce only within the firm boundaries laid down at its first forming.

Why?[3]

I have heard the following explanation in the name of Ralbag. It is only because the various species are strictly segregated that we take a hierarchical world for granted. If license were given to change identities as we choose and at will, the concept of higher and lower orders would become attenuated. It is only in a strictly hierarchical world that, as we go higher and higher, we ultimately meet up with the Ribono shel Olam. We attain an awareness of the Ribono shel Olam by moving up a ladder of *relative* values associated with various levels of being, until at last we reach the one value that is associated with the One Being Who is absolute, relative to nothing, comparable to nothing, unique beyond any uniqueness, one, incomparably one, absolutely different from any other singularity (Rambam, Yesodei HaTorah 1:4).

And that, the late, great R. Shlomo Wolbe זצ"ל teaches us,[4] introduces us to the evil seed from which *avodah zarah* develops. It feeds on the excruciating difficulty of scaling this ladder made up of various and ascending desirable qualities to its very zenith. It is so much easier to permit ourselves to become deflected along the way. All of us, as we make our way upward, tend to find values around which it seems attractive to build our world[5] and lose the will, or fail to see the need, to struggle on. For some of us it is wealth, for others power or honor. Some of us may opt for stamp collecting, others for the home team's standing.

In its essence, *avodah zarah* consists of ascribing real and lasting value to this-worldly attractions, and setting them up in competition with, or at least in addition to, the Ribono shel Olam. That is our *avodah zarah*. We do not need images to lead us astray. It is all there in our minds, undisciplined and muddle-headed as many of us are.

Avraham Avinu's tractate Avodah Zarah consisted of four hundred chapters (Avodah Zarah 14b). Ours has only five. What could Chazal possibly mean? R. Wolbe knows. After Avraham had destroyed the images in his father's store, only half the battle had been won. There were still hundreds of "strange" gods jostling for his allegiance. Each presented a different challenge; each required a different strategy. Four hundred chapters; four hundred struggles; four hundred hard-won victories. Four hundred chapters in a very difficult Masechta.

We argued above that the second *Dibra* was perhaps more alive for us than any other. We now understand why this is so. With the possible exception of the first one, the other *Dibros* apply at specific times, in specific circumstances. The prohibition against having other gods is constant and unrelenting. All of us must constantly write our own record into our own *Maseches Avodah Zarah*.

We must not forget the second half of the second *Dibra*. You will recall chapter 4, note 4, where we discussed whether the three additional prohibitions that are contained in that part of the *Dibra*[6] rise to the level of being counted as three among the 613 *mitzvos*, or whether they are to be subsumed under the general heading of *Lo Yiheyeh . . .*, and that, in effect, this second *Dibra* counts as only one *mitzvah*. This disagreement between Rambam and Ramban, important as it is, does not affect us here. The fact is that, formal *mitzvah* or not, we are forbidden to make images, to prostrate ourselves before them, and to serve them.

Most of us do not feel particularly limited by the prohibition against directing our prayers to an image or, to refine this a little, directing our prayers to the Ribono shel Olam by way of an image. From childhood we are trained how to *daven;* we know that ideally the place to *daven* is in *shul;* and we know what *shul* looks like, what is there and what is not. We have no quarrel with the second half of the second *Dibra.*

And yet, things are not so simple. Maybe we should miss the images a little more than we do.

We begin our analysis with S'forno's remarks in his introduction to Sefer VaYikra, in which he surveys the various details that, together, constitute the bringing of sacrifices in a way that is pleasing to the Ribono shel Olam. The small passage that we quote here addresses the obligation of *semichah,* the "pressing" of the hands on the animal prior to the slaughtering.

> ויסמוך את ידו על קרבנו כמתנפל ומתפלל שיהיה עונו על ראש הקרבן, כענין בשעיר המשתלח, ובזה יוציא לאיזה פועל של הכנעה את מחשבת התשובה אשר בלבו ונרצה לו לכפר עליו.
>
> He shall press his hands upon the head of the sacrifice, as someone would prostrate himself and pray that his guilt be transferred to the sacrifice.... This act of pressing the hands is a means by which he gives some physical expression to the penitence in his heart, thus eliciting goodwill and a cleansing of his sin.

Apparently, the contrition that he feels in his heart is not sufficient. He is required to give it some physical expression.[7] We tend to be impressed more by our senses than by our sense. All of us who treasure photos of our children and carry them around in our wallets can confirm this very human frailty. We know that it is the easiest thing in the world to close our eyes and conjure up the cute faces from memory. But we prefer to see the picture.[8]

There is a passage in the Kuzari that takes these ideas much, much further than anything that we would have expected from these rather tame examples. The King of the Khazars had asked the Chacham how the Ribono shel Olam could ever have forgiven the Jews for their worship of the Golden Calf. The Chacham offers some insights that can mitigate the apparently sheer heinousness of that crime.

> At that time all the nations worshipped graven images and idols, and even the philosophers who presented proofs for the unity of God could not satisfy themselves with abstract concepts, but required images . . .
>
> The Israelites looked forward to the fulfillment of Moshe's promise to bring down from heaven something tangible from God, which they could see and toward which they could turn. This would be similar to the Pillar of Cloud and the Pillar of Fire [that accompanied them] upon their Exodus from Egypt which they were able to see and toward which they were able to direct their obeisance as they bowed to God.[9]

The implications of what Kuzari is suggesting are absolutely startling. He dares to say that the Jews actually bowed toward the *Anenei Kavod* when their intention was to bow to the Ribono shel Olam! They had also hoped that the *luchos* that Moshe Rabbeinu was bringing down would serve a similar purpose. All this, after they had heard the second *Dibra* forty days earlier, that physical portrayals were interdicted and after they had heard (Shemos 20:20) the prohibition against making any kind of image to serve as an intermediary between themselves and the Ribono shel Olam (see chapter 6). There is certainly no indication of any kind that the Kuzari was in any way critical of this usage.

My purpose in citing this astounding passage is not to examine the halachic aspects of this usage. Clearly there must be some significant differences between, on the one hand, the clouds and the *luchos,* both of which, to some degree, bear a divine imprint and, on the other hand, man-made objects. To find and define that difference falls outside the purview of this essay. I cite it only in order to demonstrate the urgent need to have something tangible to help them along in their prayers that the people apparently felt.

We too are human, and we too would probably find it a great help if we were allowed to have something physical to stand in for the intangibles upon which we are asked to focus. We live in a culture in which loyalty to one's flag has fallen into disrepute. But we must recall that there were times when people thought otherwise. Those of us who live in America can, through the medium of the national anthem, refresh our memory of the sheer inspiration that people were able to draw from that simple piece of cloth adorned by stripes and stars. People knew that it was no more than a symbol, but, as a lowly symbol it still worked its magic.

Our attachment to the physical is powerful, indeed.

And the Torah, in the second half of the second *Dibra,* denies us this seemingly harmless aid. Here is what the Torah itself has to say in explanation of this prohibition: *Watch yourself very carefully, since you did not see any image on the day that God spoke to you out of the fire, at Chorev. You shall therefore not become corrupt and make a statue depicting any symbol. [Do not make] any male or female image. Nor the image of any animal...* (Devarim 4:15–17).[10]

... Since you did not see any image on the day that God spoke to you out of the fire, at Chorev. Apparently, images are prohibited to us since none was used at Sinai. But is this fair reasoning? It is true that there was no image, but there were many other physical manifestations. There were the clouds and the thunder and the lightning and the shofar blasts. Clearly the form

that the Sinaitic experience took recognized human limitations and took consideration of the fact that, within those limitations, these physical accompaniments could and would play a significant role.

It seems to me that this question forces us to understand the verse as follows.[11] You must realize that, even though I permitted a certain amount of physicality to intrude upon your experience of *Matan Torah,* this indulgence stopped short of permitting an actual image.

In practical terms that leaves us, let us say at an ordinary weekday Minchah, very much to our own devices. A make-or-break business deal may lie in the offing, a difficult and decisive test may loom in the near future, I may have had a fight with my wife or received a stern note from the principal, my mind may be darting hither and yon in all kinds of different directions, and there is nothing that can help me. No thunder, no lightning, and certainly no image.[12]

I believe that it is here that the second half of the second *Dibra* earns its *Dibra* standing. It demands much more from us than to simply avoid making or worshipping idols. It demands that we liberate ourselves from cloying smallness, that we become masters of our mind and powers of concentration. It is not too much to ask from citizens in a *Mamleches Kohanim VeGoy Kadosh.*

ELEVEN

The Third Dibra

לא תשא את שם ה' אלהיך לשאו . . . , *Do not take the name of HaShem your God in vain . . .*

This third *Dibra* is counted as a *mitzvah* by the Rambam in his Sefer HaMitzvos, Negative Commands 62. It forbids invoking God's name in an oath where no purpose is served.

Here is the background. A *shevu'ah* is an oath. It is a formula that is used to lend credibility to either an affirmation or a denial, above and beyond the value that would have been ascribed to the proposition in question, had it not been couched in the language of *shevu'ah.* This additional claim to credence derives from the fact that the *shevu'ah* somehow invokes the Ribono shel Olam[1] to bolster the trust that the statement deserves.

Of course there are such things as false oaths. A person may couch his assertion in the form of a *shevu'ah* and still be telling a lie. That is a heinous crime, interdicted by the Torah,[2] but that is not the immediate[3] subject of this *Dibra.* Our *Dibra* deals with an *unnecessary* (not a false) use of the *shevu'ah* formula. Examples are, using the *shevu'ah* either to affirm something that is obviously true—this stone is made of stone—or obviously untrue—this stone is made of gold. In either case the Ribono shel Olam was invoked frivolously. It added no credence to what was asserted, either because the fact was anyway self-evident, or because it was obviously untrue.

As we now turn to an analysis of why this particular *mitzvah* was considered fundamental enough to be included in *Aseres HaDibros,* we may as well begin with a question that has probably already occurred to you, dear Reader. It is this. Why, if the misuse of the *shevu'ah* formula belongs among the *Aseres HaDibros,* would it be the needless *shevu'ah* rather than the false *shevu'ah* that is included? I suspect that all of us would judge the false oath to be a more serious dereliction than the needless one. Why, then, choose the one over the other?

I will introduce our discussion with an observation that struck me only recently. Any youngster who is educated in our school system where Mishnah and Gemara appear in the curriculum around fourth or fifth grade, knows from a very early age, and takes for granted for the rest of his life, that certain cases are decided in Beis Din on the strength of oaths taken by the litigants. Where the conditions are right, no litigant can protest that he is not obliged to trust his opponent's oath. Oaths are imposed by Beis Din and will be believed.

I wondered whether there is an equivalent to that in secular law. I knew that witnesses are "sworn in" before they testify. But are any cases decided on the strength of an oath taken by a litigant to bolster his claim? I called a law professor friend to ask, and he told me that to the best of his knowledge no such usage exists.

I wondered why this should be so.

Let us get back to our main topic. The first matter that requires our attention is to get a good definition. What exactly is a *shevu'ah*? I make a promise that I will do a certain thing. In the end, I don't do it. I have broken my promise. That is certainly not recommended. I lose a lot of credibility; people will no longer trust me as they did in the past. But, at the end of the day, I have not committed a particularly dreadful crime. If instead of having said, "I promise," I said, "I swear," everything is ratcheted upward. I have set the entire universe atrembling (note 3). I have done something truly dreadful, to the point that God Himself testifies that He will not be able to find it in His heart to forgive me.[4]

What have I done?

Above, I indicated that the higher degree of credibility that accrues to a proposition that is couched in the form of an oath comes about because, in some way, a *shevu'ah* invokes the Ribono shel Olam to bolster its claim to be the truth. The time has come to explain what I meant by that. How does the Ribono shel Olam enter into the picture?[5]

I had always assumed that a *shevu'ah* somehow ties the truth of the assertion to the truth of the Ribono shel Olam. "This assertion is as true as the Ribono shel Olam is true." That, of course, would explain the utmost seriousness of swearing falsely. If what I am saying is false, that would constitute a denial of the Ribono shel Olam. No wonder the world trembled at the thought (see note 3). However, that interpretation seems to be impossible in the light of Teshuvas Radbaz 17. He was asked if a person said, "Just as God is true, so also is this assertion true," whether this would constitute a *shevu'ah*. He answered:

> To speak thus is a dreadful sin. It comes close to constituting heresy. It would be appropriate to speak harshly to the person who used this expression and to instruct him that such words are sinful. I would even recommend that it would be appropriate to thrash him until he repents on what he said . . . for under no circumstances would it be permitted to make any comparison between the truth of the Ribono shel Olam and the truth of any of His creatures,[6] even if what he claims is true. This person deserves to be punished. Woe to him for having done . . .[7]

So what exactly is a *shevu'ah*? What does the word mean and how does the use of that expression bolster the level of credibility of whatever it is that is being asserted?

There is a grammatical anomaly that thickens the mystery. Instinct would certainly tell us that the active voice would be appropriate in using the verb "to swear." That is what we do in English and in the few languages of which I have some knowledge. Nevertheless, in *Lashon HaKodesh,* the verb appears only in the *niph'al,* the passive voice. We do not say, *"ani shove'a,"* I swear, but *"ani nishba,"* I am being . . . what? I suppose that the answer to that would be, "I am putting myself in the situation of being bound by an oath." But what does that mean? Why not say simply, "I swear"?

The root from which the verb "to swear" is formed is, of course, *shin-beis-ayin,* which we know from *sheva,* the number seven. Is there a connection between this number and a *shevu'ah*?

R. Samson Rafael Hirsch says "Yes!" and demonstrates that this connection is quite specifically made in Chumash. At Bereishis 21:22 and onward we have the story of Avimelech's visit to Avraham. In that passage the word *sheva,* seven, and *shevu'ah,* oath, are freely intermingled—most blatantly in verse 31, *Therefore he called that place, Be'er Sheva, for both of them had sworn there*—and it becomes perfectly clear that the two concepts are connected. R. Hirsch invokes the inner significance of the number seven. Of course we cannot think of seven without thinking of Shabbos, and can readily reach the conclusion that seven is that number that testifies to God's connection to our physical world. During the six days of Creation, a theoretical observer might have concluded that no such connection exists. Shabbos disabuses him of this error.

From there R. Hirsch moves on to his explanation of the passive form that the verb takes in *Lashon HaKodesh. Ani nishba* would mean that *I recognize myself as being subordinate to the "seven" concept.* My property is mine because the Ribono shel Olam allows it to be mine. I willingly submit it all to the Ribono shel Olam, asking Him to take all of it away from me if what I am saying is not true.

I believe that the data that R. Hirsch uses to reach his conclusion can equally well be employed to explain the concept of *shevu'ah* somewhat differently. Instead of explaining the passive form as pointing to an act of subordination—opening the path that would lead to an appropriate punishment if what is being asserted were false—I would suggest that we can translate *ani nishba* more literally and without recourse to introducing the somewhat extraneous issue of how a false oath might be punished. I would render *ani nishba* as, quite literally, *I am "besevened" as I make this assertion. I know full well that the Ribono shel Olam is somehow present in this world since that is what the number seven conveys to us, and that what I am saying is being said in His presence. You can be quite certain that, this given, I would not tell anything other than the absolute truth.*

The heinousness of making a false assertion after such an introduction needs no elaboration. The person who is swearing falsely is really saying, "I know that the Ribono shel Olam is listening, but I do not care." Things do not get much worse than that.

I believe that we now understand by what right forbidden oaths make it into *Aseres HaDibros*. They certainly have a vast array of implications beyond their *mitzvah* status. They demand a constant awareness of the Ribono shel Olam's immanence right down here in our physical world. This awareness surely belongs among the constituent underpinnings of a *Mamleches Kohanim VeGoy Kadosh*.

We asked how we could explain why the needless, frivolous oath was included in *Aseres HaDibros* rather than the false oath. It seems to me that the very assumption I made when I asked the question will now serve us to justify the answer. I had assumed that the false oath is a more heinous crime than the frivolous oath. That is true and it is for that same reason that it is just the lesser evil that makes it into *Aseres HaDibros*. The fact that even this lesser evil rises to a level that justifies its inclusion in the ten most basic requirements that must be met if we are to deserve the title of a *Mamleches Kohanim VeGoy Kadosh* shows just how demanding this level of relationship to the Ribono shel Olam can be. To tell us that God will never forgive one who misuses His majesty in order to make a false *shevu'ah* is one thing. To extend that same measure of heinousness to a simple lack of earnestness that, at the end of the day, harmed nobody, is quite another.[8]

To be the *segulah* of the Ribono shel Olam, to be His *Mamleches Kohanim VeGoy Kadosh*, is no small matter.

It makes me feel good to contemplate that apparently in no other system than our own are litigations decided on the strength of a *shevu'ah* made by one of the litigants. The Ribono shel Olam knows His own. He trusts us because we have earned His trust.

TWELVE

The Fourth Dibra

זכור את יום השבת לקדשו . . . , *Remember the Shabbos day to declare it holy . . .*

I was afraid that this essay was going to be either too long or too short. I reasoned that there is so much available material on Shabbos that is accessible to everyone in books, in articles, on tape, and in videos, that either I would attempt to distill all or most of it—too long—or just give up and leave this *Dibra* out altogether—too short. As I thought things over, I discovered that my fears were ungrounded. It turned out that within the system in which I am trying to work, attempting to separate the "*Dibra*" element from the "*mitzvah*" element, there was still some acreage left to be plowed. What I discovered while I was researching this essay was entirely new to me. I hope that the material is close enough to the truth to be acceptable, and that it is also new, stimulating, and interesting for you, dear Reader.

The *mitzvah* that begins the fourth *Dibra* commands us to sanctify Shabbos by making Kiddush on Friday night.[1] It is counted by the Rambam in his Sefer HaMitzvos, Positive Mitzvos 155. As we have done for the first three *Dibros,* we will now attempt to discover what gives this particular *mitzvah* its *Dibra* standing.[2]

I suspect that most of you, dear Readers, will agree that the following question needs asking. I think that most of us, upon hearing that Shabbos is included in *Aseres HaDibros,* would have assumed that this inclusion would be limited to the prohibition against working on Shabbos. For most of us, that is the "real" Shabbos. The obligation to make Kiddush seems somehow peripheral. It does not at all seem to define the day. I think that all of us would have been perfectly happy if Kiddush had not been part of *Aseres HaDibros* but would have been left to some other part of the Torah.[3] And yet, it is given pride of place as the opening sentence of the *Dibra.* Why is that?

Let us begin our analysis by asking ourselves what is behind this obligation of "sanctifying" Shabbos. Shabbos owes us nothing and its sanctity exists entirely independently of anything that we might or might not do. One would have supposed that the Ribono shel Olam's "Kiddush," the one He made on the very first Shabbos, is the only one that really counts: *And God blessed the seventh day* AND SANCTIFIED IT, *for it was with this day that He withdrew from all His labors which God had called into being with the intention of developing it further* (Bereishis 2:3).[4] After that, it seems that any act of sanctification that we might undertake would be irrelevant.

The key to the solution of this conundrum may lie in the wording of the *Amidah* that we recite on Shabbos morning. In the passage that begins with the words *Yismach Moshe be'matnas chelko,* we read,

ושני לוחות אבנים הוריד בידו
וכתוב בהם שמירת שבת
וכן כתוב בתורתיך.

He brought down two tablets made from stone,
The obligation to guard Shabbos was engraved upon them,
And thus too is it written in the Torah.

Why is the last line of interest to us? Think about it. What is so important about the fact that Shabbos appears not only as a *Dibra* among *Aseres HaDibros,* but also as a regular part of the Torah?[5] Does this really affect us in any way?

Well, let us see.

The passage that is referenced to show where Shabbos is mentioned in the Torah is Shemos 31:16–18.

ושמרו בני ישראל את השבת
Let then the Benei Yisrael keep the Shabbos
לעשות את השבת לדרתם ברית עולם
. . .
ביני ובין בני ישראל אות הוא לעלם . . .
It is an eternal sign between Me and the Benei Yisrael . . .

I have left the center phrase untranslated because everything we are trying to learn will depend upon how we treat this difficult wording. What exactly can *la'asos es HaShabbos,* to "make" the Shabbos, mean? Ibn Ezra is forthright in his questioning. How does Shabbos involve action? It is a day of resting, of "not doing," the very antitheses of *la'asos*? To avoid this difficulty, he suggests that this phrase refers to what we must do *before* Shabbos in order to make sure that the Shabbos rest will not be disturbed. For example, meals are to be prepared before Shabbos, extended travel is to be avoided, and so on. We "keep" the Shabbos *on* Shabbos, by "making" it *before* Shabbos.[6]

S'forno has a different approach and it his idea that I would now like to consider. Here are his words.

ושמרו בני ישראל את השבת בעולם הזה,
לעשות את השבת ביום שכלו שבת.

The Benei Yisrael are to keep Shabbos in this world,
in order to create (make) Shabbos for the future, a Shabbos that will be eternal.[7]

If I understand S'forno correctly, these few, seemingly simple words can literally change lives. He proposes nothing less than that, on Shabbos, we ourselves, each one for his or her self, creates their own Olam HaBa. As we keep Shabbos we are building a home for ourselves wherein we will spend eternity—a long, never-ending Shabbos.

What a thought!

Now, S'forno does not make the following point, but I suspect that it is what he had in mind. Berachos 57b teaches that Shabbos is *me'ein Olam HaBa,* that it embodies elements of Olam HaBa. Given that, it seems to me to make sense to reason that the way I spend my time on Shabbos, the degree to which I am awake to its whisperings, how I carry myself, the words I speak and the words I do not speak, all tell some very revealing stories concerning my suitability as a citizen of Olam HaBa. Shabbos is speaking to me, am I listening? Do I know how to appreciate its magnificent offerings or am I focused on my nap? Would an "*Olam HaBa-dicker Yid*" want to spend Shabbos at my house or would he not? Would he feel that he had met a kindred spirit or would he look at me pityingly as an illiterate alien in the world of Shabbos?

It is a sobering thought, is it not? How many of us would be happy to learn that Shabbos, as we spend it today, will serve as a blueprint for our eternity. Even as I am typing this I am shuddering. There is a lot about our lives that we need to fix.

We asked earlier what the point of our Kiddush might be. Shabbos has its own sanctity gifted it by God; what need does it have for my puny willingness to add my assent? We have an answer now—in spades. To tell the truth, I am ashamed for having asked. Of course Shabbos has its own objective sanctity, dating from that first, cosmic Kiddush that the Ribono shel Olam made in Eden. The Kiddush that we are called upon to make tests the degree to which we are listening for and to, that *ur*-Kiddush that the Ribono shel Olam made so long ago. Who is making Kiddush at my Shabbos table? Is it my mouth or is it my heart? Do I have any spiritual faculties left that can pick up the sacred vibes, or have they been drowned and vitiated by untold gallons of *cholent*?

In the earlier part of this essay, I used the word "peripheral" in describing how many of us might view the opening *mitzvah* of the fourth *Dibra*. Now we know the truth. It is not peripheral at all. It stands at the very center of Shabbos. It is what lifts it beyond the *mitzvah* category, into that of the *Dibra*. It, perhaps more than any other of the *Dibros*, tests our mettle. What kind of Shabbos are we ushering in?[8] I spoke earlier of citizenship in Olam HaBa. We really have a more immediate problem about which to worry. How suited are we to make it as a citizen in a *Mamleches Kohanim VeGoy Kadosh*?

And finally I think that I can offer a reasonable explanation for the wording of our Shabbos morning *Amidah*. We asked why the fact that a *Dibra* that was engraved upon the *luchos* appears also in the Torah is of such significance. Here is why. In the case of Shabbos, the difference between *mitzvah* and *Dibra* is blurred. The *Dibra* concept of creating our own Olam HaBa that is expressed in the *mitzvah* to make

Kiddush is so integral to the idea of Shabbos the *me'ein Olam HaBa,* that even when Shabbos is mentioned in the rest of the Torah, it comes wrapped in that same idea. When we consider the *VeShamru* passage in Ki Sisa, it seems to us that the phrase "*thereby creating Shabbos for the future*" was not really required in that context. It expresses a philosophy rather than an obligation, a philosophy that, as we have now explained, is already expressed in *Aseres HaDibros*. Why repeat it? The answer can only be that Shabbos is what it is. It comes in only one size. We must try to make it fit, or, better still, to make us fit it.

THIRTEEN

The Fifth Dibra

כבד את אביך ואת אמך..., *Honor your father and your mother...*

This *mitzvah* that obliges us to honor our parents is counted by the Rambam as Positive Mitzvos 210 in his Sefer HaMitzvos. As we did with the earlier *Dibros,* we will attempt to examine what aspect of this *mitzvah* might have lifted it to the level of a *Dibra.*

Mitzvah 211, there, spells out our obligation to stand in awe before our parents (VaYikra 19:3). Inevitably, as we go along, it will occur to us to ask why the one, but not the other, belongs among the *Dibros.* There seems to be no apparent logic that would demand that we include the one but not the other. The differences between honoring and fearing are spelled out for us in Kiddushin 31b and, at the most simple level, can be classified as dealing respectively with positives and negatives. Honoring obliges us, among various other similar gestures, to help our parents by feeding and clothing them, while fearing them forbids us to sit in their seats, contradict them, and the like. That difference should not militate against including both among *Aseres HaDibros.* The fourth *Dibra,* Shabbos, contains both the positive (Kiddush) and the negative (refrain from identified *melachos*). Why should this not work just as well for the fifth?

As I was sitting at my computer wondering how to continue, I found my mind drifting to the term "nuclear family." I have the feeling that the idea is of fairly recent vintage,[1] but now that it has become a part of the English language, it seems to pop up quite frequently. The point of all this is to admit that till a couple of minutes ago, I had no idea what it meant. Obviously "nuclear" has an ominous sound to it, and without knowing exactly how, I associated it with some kind of explosion. After looking around, I discovered that it is not at all threatening. Apparently "nuclear" in this compound noun has the meaning of *basic, cardinal, central,* and the entirely innocent expression is used to describe the basic family, consisting of father, mother, and child(ren). It is used as a contrast to the "extended family," which might include uncles, aunts, cousins, and so on.

So let us think about the nuclear family, the parents and children who populate the fifth *Dibra*. How, within a *Mamleches Kohanim VeGoy Kadosh*, the two generations involved arrange their relationships with each other seems to be of primary importance to the Ribono shel Olam. As we go along, we will find that the need for such a relationship will ultimately explain how and why this *mitzvah* rises to the level of a *Dibra*. Let us see where all this is going to lead us.

Our first stop will be in *parashas* Noso (BeMidbar 5:5–6:21), where against all expectations the narrative is interrupted by three major blocks of *halachah* that would have fit perfectly into Sefer VaYikra, but seem incongruous where they in fact appear. They are: *gezel ha'ger*, the laws governing property that was stolen from a proselyte who has now died and has left no heirs; *Sotah*, the laws governing a married woman who is suspected of having committed adultery; and *Nazir*, the laws governing a person who seeks an appropriate form of asceticism, to help him experience a greater closeness to the Ribono shel Olam.

Ramban explains that each of these three blocks deals with issues that arise from the counting of the Jews and the formalizing of the camping arrangements that had been described in *parashas* BeMidbar. In his view it is highly appropriate that these *halachos* appear precisely where they are.

We will address only *Sotah*, the centre block. Here is how Ramban views the logic of recording these *halachos* here.

> ולא נזכרה מנחת הסוטה עם שאר המנחות בתורת כהנים . . . בעבור שיחס את העם לבית אבותם, נתן להם דת ודין לדעת הממזרים שאינם בני בעלי אמותם כאשר יבא חשד בלב האיש על אשתו.
>
> The sacrifices that are to be brought in conjunction with the investigation of the *Sotah* are listed here rather than in VaYikra together with all the other sacrifices. They belong here in BeMidbar, directly after the census was taken, because that census was organized around the family unit. This indicates that the family is the building

block from which Klal Yisrael is structured.[2] It therefore became necessary to install a system through which the integrity of the family unit could be protected and *mamzeirim* identified.[3]

Our nuclear family has suddenly taken a giant step upward in our rating system. We must tread carefully here because we are treading on holy ground. It seems clear from this Ramban that the *Mamleches Kohanim VeGoy Kadosh* is less a conglomeration of individuals than it is a conglomeration of families. Note well! A family is a unit in which the attitude that two generations have toward each other looms large in significance.

Note well once more! As individuals, our "vertical" connections are stronger and more significant than our "horizontal" ones. It is our relationship to our father that ultimately leads us back to the Avos. It is our relationship to our children that reaches into the future and makes sure that one day, even if only by proxy through our descendants, we will be part of the crowd that will go out to welcome Melech HaMoshiach.

At this point I would like to refer to a brilliant insight that I learned from the late R. Mordechai Miller ז"ל, a mentor and friend from my early Gateshead experience, for many years Principal of the Gateshead Jewish Teacher's Seminary. I refer to a passage in his *sefer*, Olas Shabbat BeShabbato, in his second essay on *parashas* BeMidbar. R. Miller is intrigued by two details that, as Chazal teach it, were part of the drama at Sinai, and, as can be seen from various Midrashic sources, appear somehow to have been connected.[4] The first is the well-known Chazal that the Ribono shel Olam suspended Mount Sinai over the people like a gigantic barrel and told them that if they were to refuse to accept the Torah, they would be buried beneath the mountain.

The second, less well known Chazal is that the Ribono shel Olam was willing to give us His Torah only after we had been able to produce genealogical documentation that we were indeed children of the Avos.[5] In fact, according to one Midrashic source, the non-Jews were denied the Torah only because they were unable to produce such genealogical proof.[6]

As stated above, R. Miller marshals proof that the two are connected. Genealogical documentation was required *because* the intention was to force the issue by threatening the Jews as they were huddled beneath the mountain.

What does one have to do with the other?

R. Miller has recourse to the Rambam in Hilchos Geirushin 2:20. A *get*, a bill of divorce, is only valid if the husband grants it of his own free will. If he is forced to give it, the *get* is not valid. However, there are situations in which the wife has a halachic warrant to demand a *get*. If the husband proves to be obdurate and refuses to comply with his obligation, we force him—to say, "I want!" Now, if ever there was a legal fiction, this would appear to be it. Are we not deceiving ourselves when we claim that this *get* was given willingly? Is there really a meaningful difference between forcing the husband to give the *get* (invalid) and forcing him to assert that he wants to give it when he really does not (valid)?

Rambam maintains that, indeed, there is a great and valid distinction between the two.

> ולמה לא בטל גט זה שהרי הוא אנוס בין ביד גוים בין ביד ישראל שאין אומרין אנוס אלא למי שנלחץ ונדחק לעשות דבר שאינו מחוייב מן התורה לעשותו. כגון מי שהוכה עד שמכר או נתן. אבל מי שתקפו יצרו הרע לבטל מצוה או לעשות עבירה והוכה עד שעשה דבר שחייב לעשותו או עד שנתרחק מדבר שאסור לעשותו אין זה אנוס ממנו אלא הוא אנס עצמו בדעתו הרעה. לפיכך זה שאינו רוצה לגרש מאחר שהוא רוצה להיות מישראל רוצה הוא לעשות כל המצות ולהתרחק מן העבירות ויצרו הוא שתקפו. וכיון שהוכה עד שתשש יצרו ואמר רוצה אני כבר גרש לרצונו.
>
> Now, why, in this instance, is the *get* not invalid? After all, at the end of the day, he *was* forced to give it? . . .
>
> The answer is that we only consider a person to have acted under duress when he had no halachic obligation to do that thing. For example if someone were to force a landowner to sell his field where he has no obligation to do so. However, when he is halachically obliged to do

> this thing and he refuses to do so, then, on the contrary, our assumption is that, in as much as he wants to maintain his status as a good Jew, he would really want to do what is right. It is his Yetzer HaRa who denies him the freedom to act according to his conscience. Under those circumstances, when we apply force, we are exerting duress upon the Yetzer HaRa, not upon him. When he says, "I want!" these words reflect the real truth. He simply needed our help to permit him to slip out from under the Yetzer HaRa's coercive tactics.[7]

R. Miller finds the solution to his problem in this Rambam. Clearly, the suspension of the mountain over the people is an act of coercion. As such, it would be meaningless if one were not able to count on an inner core of goodness that would make Rambam's argument applicable. That inner core existed, but it existed only because we were able to trace our descent from the *Avos*. Be the necessity of resorting to the suspension of the mountain what it may.[8] Once it was a necessary part of *Matan Torah,* the other nations were excluded by definition.

We are now ready to return to our nuclear family of whom we observed that they are the units of which Klal Yisrael is composed.[9] We further concluded that, from this insight, it follows that vertical ties are more significant than any horizontal ones. We are now ready to appreciate the significance of these discoveries. It is only through the "son to father" tie, that as we go further and further back, our *sefer yuchasin* ultimately leads us back to the Avos.

We are who and what we are because the Ribono shel Olam trusted us with His Torah. No wonder that the command to honor our parents who pave the way back to our roots belongs among *Aseres HaDibros,* the constituent underpinnings of our status as a *Mamleches Kohanim VeGoy Kadosh.*

There is another aspect to the father/son relationship, no less significant than the one that we have just explored. Let us go to Devarim 4:9 to learn the Torah's plan for keeping the Torah's teachings alive for us throughout the generations.

רק השמר לך ושמר נפשך מאד פן תשכח את הדברים אשר ראו עיניך ופן יסורו מלבבך כל ימי חייך והודעתם לבניך ולבני בניך. יום אשר עמדת לפני ה' אלהיך בחרב . . .

Only take heed and watch yourself very carefully, so that you do not forget the things that your eyes saw. Do not let [this memory] leave your hearts all the days of your lives. Teach your children and your children's children about the day you stood before HaShem your God at Chorev . . .[10]

This verse spells out very clearly what the Ribono shel Olam teaches us concerning the most potent antidote against allowing the basic principles that define our Jewishness to slip away from us. It is *Mesorah,* the *passing on* of these truths to our children and grandchildren.

In order to enable us to fully absorb the profound wisdom of this verse, it is worthwhile to study a few lines of the Ramban on that passage.

. . . כי כשנעתיק גם כן הדבר לבנינו ידעו שהיה הדבר אמת בלא ספק כאלו ראוהו כל הדורות, כי לא נעיד שקר לבנינו ולא ננחיל אותם דבר הבל ואין בם מועיל והם לא יסתפקו כלל בעדותנו שנעיד להם, אבל יאמינו בודאי שראינו כולנו בעינינו.

[The earlier part of the Ramban explains why the Sinai experience is such a vital part of our Jewish heritage. He then continues to explain why it is so crucial that we pass on these truths to our children:] . . . for when we pass on these matters to our children, they will know that all that we tell them is the absolute truth, without the slightest doubt. It will be as though all the generations had themselves stood at Sinai and seen what happened there with their own eyes. They will know all this with such certainty because they are convinced that we would not bear false witness to our children, nor would we pass on to them stupid traditions that help nobody. They will have absolutely no doubts concerning what we tell them but will believe us with absolute trust that all these are occurrences that we witnessed with our own eyes.

This is a powerful Ramban, is it not? However, we will be excused for asking ourselves, "Is it true?" Does our experience really confirm that children believe their parents uncritically and absolutely? Of course we all know that it is not so. We live in a benighted generation in which fathers have ceased to play their true role as respected, awe-inspiring, and loving educators and rather pathetically attempt to become their children's friends.[11] Family relationships have been turned inside out and upside down and nothing is anymore as it should be.[12, 13]

Let us think back to better times. There are major halachic opinions that the *mitzvah* of honoring our parents goes beyond the examples listed in the Gemara. It includes the obligation to *truly respect his parents in his heart and to consider them among the important and most honored personages in the community, even if they are not generally viewed as such* (Chayei Adam 67:3 taken from Sefer Chareidim).

These authorities go so far as to say that the fifth *Dibra* even obliges us to love our parents even as they love us.[14]

In the light of these rulings, we can understand Ramban very well. When relationships between parents and children are as they should be, when the fifth *Dibra* is allowed to work its magic, then the *Mesorah* can indeed guarantee that the Sinaitic experience will remain alive for us and our children to all eternity.

As a finale to this rather involved, but in my view very rewarding, chapter, we can attempt an answer to the question with which we began. Why does the *mitzvah* of honoring our parents make it into *Aseres HaDibros* but not the *mitzvah* of standing in awe before them? As we have worked things out, the answer seems quite simple. It is the respect that we feel for them in our hearts, our conviction that they are *among the most important and most honored personages in the community* that create the relationship that allows our parents to function as the links that take us back to the Avos and allows our children to carry us forward toward Melech HaMoshiach. These aspects of parenthood are vested in the positive actions that are mandated by the obligation to honor, rather than in the prohibitions that are part of the obligation to fear.

FOURTEEN

The Sixth Dibra I

לא תרצח, *Do not murder.*

This *mitzvah* that forbids us to take a life, except in a legitimate war or where it is otherwise mandated by the *halachah,* is counted by the Rambam in his Sefer HaMitzvos, Negative Commands 289. Once more, it will be our challenge to discover what elements in this *mitzvah* lift it to the level of a *Dibra*. This time, though, it looks as if we will not have an easy job. The sheer evil of taking an innocent life seems so obvious; it is so universally condemned that the prohibition seems well able to stand on its own. Why philosophize about the obvious? What values might there be that are not covered by the simple, magisterial *Lo tirzach*! Any embellishment would seem to undercut the self-assured brevity of two simple words. Why not leave well enough alone?

Well, you, dear Reader, will be able to answer that last question once you have read this essay. I have the feeling that there are some potentially rich seams that we ought to track and then to mine.

A good place to start our search would be the point at which the Ribono shel Olam reveals himself to No'ach after the *mabul* (Bereishis 9:1–8). There He tells No'ach that henceforth he will be allowed to kill animals and eat their meat.[1] Verses 5 and 6 then stress that that license to kill animals would not extend to killing people. *He who sheds the blood of man, his blood shall be shed by man. [Man's life is sacrosanct] because God created man in the divine image* (TSELEM ELOHIM).[2] At that point in history the sanction against murdering is based upon the fact that man is created in God's "image." What exactly does that mean? For that we go to Sefer HaIkarim 1:11.

ויובן מזה ג"כ שידיעת השם מקפת בדברים האישיים ובדברים הכלליים ולהורות ע"ז תמצא כי כשהקב"ה נגלה על בני נח שופך דם האדם באדם דמו ישפך כי בצלם אלהים עשה את האדם (בראשית ט') לרמוז על שהידיעה הפרטית דבקה באדם. שאם לא היתה בו ידיעה **כללית כמו בשאר ב"ח לשמור המין בלבד** מה טעם שיהרג הרצח. וכי

> ההורג אדם אחד הוא הורג כל המין אבל יאמר כי לפי שנעשה אדם בצלם אלהים הנה הוא קיים באיש וההורגו ראוי לעונש אחר שהידיעה האלהית הפרטיית דבקה בו מצד הכח השכלי אשר בו כעליונים אשר הם קיימים באיש והידיעה הפרטיית דבקה בהם מצד הכח השכלי שבהם וע"כ היה האדם ראוי לשכר ולעונש הפרטי המיועד בתורה.
>
> Ikarim sets out to demonstrate that people, as opposed to animals, have individual worth. It would not occur to anybody that killing an animal would carry the death penalty, but murdering a person does. The explanation must be that animals are valued only as part of a species. As long as the species remains, the death of the individual animal has no significance. Every human being, because of the uniqueness of his soul, is, so to speak, a species of one.[3] When he is murdered, that whole species has disappeared forever.

There we have it. Each human is an entire species. He is unique. There is none like him. He cannot be replaced. The crime of killing him is heinous, beyond any other.

That sounds simple enough and we now have to make a decision. Do we stop here or do we soldier on? It seems to me that we still have much unfinished business. Let us take the challenge and see where it will lead us.

Here comes a rather silly question, but sometimes silly questions can also serve a very serious purpose. How unique is unique? Are there levels of uniqueness? If I recall my schooldays correctly, quantifying uniqueness in expressions like "very unique" earned us, at the very least, a verbal rap on the knuckles from a frustrated English teacher.[4] And yet, and yet, I wish to argue that, indeed, in very special circumstances, there may be differences in the degree of uniqueness after all.

My point of departure is the Sefer HaIkarim that we have just learned. The seriousness of the crime of murder is rooted in the uniqueness of each individual; ergo, since uniqueness cannot be graded, each murder should be considered equally abhorrent. I will argue that that may not be strictly true.

As I was thinking about the uniqueness that inheres in the *Tselem Elohim,* my mind drifted to Avos 3:15 where R. Akiva speaks of three levels of love that the Ribono shel Olam showed toward humankind. "Man" is beloved because he was created *"betselem"*; "Israel" is beloved because God refers to them as "His children"; Israel is further beloved because God gifted them with a "magnificent gift" (the Torah), which He had used as a blueprint for creating the world.[5]

I have always been puzzled by the third category. I understand fully, or at least I think I do, why giving us the Torah is described as a gesture of love. We recall from the Midrash that God gave us His Torah over the very fierce objections of His Mal'achim. They felt that the Torah did not belong among humankind who, because of their propensity to sin, could easily debase it. So the Ribono shel Olam loved us enough to trust us with His most precious possession. But what about the fact that God had used it as a blueprint for creating the world? That aspect of the Torah seems irrelevant to us. Since we have no worlds to create, it would seem that this particular faculty with which the Torah is endowed would not be particularly useful to us.

Or would it? Let us ask ourselves what might be meant by the assertion that the Ribono shel Olam used the Torah as a blueprint to create the world. We have all learned Torah and found nothing in it that we could translate into the energies that make things hum down here. There is no hint of a potency that can conjure the tender, fragrant lily out of the ground, or growl[6] the threatening thunderclap out of the sky. In short, there is nothing that seems even remotely connected with creating worlds.

So what did R. Akiva mean when he told us that it was by the Torah that the Ribono shel Olam created the world?

I suppose that it must mean that a measure of equivalency exists in the world of the spirit to the myriad modes of manifestations that we experience in our physical world. Let us take the simple word "big." We know precisely what that means down here, but also realize that in a different world, one in which brute size is meaningless, there is the concept "great" that, in terms of that world, expresses the very same thing. We can also turn this thought around and maintain that our physical world is modeled after a higher world, of the spirit. There are those who claim that this is the real explanation for the apparent anthropomorphisms that occur so frequently in the Torah. We are used to think that the Hebrew "*yad*" is a hand and that when the Torah speaks of the "*yad*" of the Ribono shel Olam, it is anthropomorphism, using a physical concept in connection with God, where it is totally inappropriate, as a kind of *mashal* to help us understand a difficult concept. Clearly, we can also turn this on its head and maintain that *yad* is an expression denoting divine power and that our hand is called a *yad* as a kind of *mashal* to help us understand a difficult concept.

When Raban Gamliel predicted (Shabbos 30b) that one day Eretz Yisrael will bring forth ready-made rolls and fine woolen clothes, he knew of what he spoke. Our present world is indeed a *mashal* for a higher, more spiritual one, but it falls very short of expressing the entire range of possibilities that prevail up there. When Moshiach comes we will get a much truer picture of what is really the will of the Ribono shel Olam. R. Chaninah ben Dosa is the one who formulated the aphorism that says it all. "The God Who decreed that oil should burn can just as easily decree that vinegar should burn" (Ta'anis 25a).

Once that is understood, then, maybe, just maybe, the Torah's faculty to serve as the blueprint for a very physical earth can after all turn out to be very useful to us. The late great R. Wolbe writes in his HeAdam Bi'Yekar, that if we are going to devote our lives to assure that our very physical bodies will be ready to arise at *Techiyas HaMeisim*, we had better be certain to teach that body the language that will be spoken there. All our petty cravings for objects that lie outside ourselves will find no resonance in a place that values only inwardness.[7] We need to discover the secrets of building a world down here that, at the very least, has diplomatic relations with Olam HaBa. God help us if it turns out that we require a visa.

Let us formulate what we have now learned. Our bodies are, or at least appear to be, our own little fiefdoms. The difference between our "world" and His world lies in who (or Who) is in charge. The Ribono shel Olam runs the world out there. We are the exclusive *ba'alei batim* of the lives that we build for ourselves. We decide to what our ears will be attuned; whether to the light, attractive siren-song of things, or to the profound, deeply moving, deeply disturbing sound of silence.[8]

It is time to return to our silly little discussion of the graded uniqueness. We are all unique. The question is how that uniqueness will express itself. It can be manifest in our standing as an "Adam" drafting all our faculties to better the physical world (R. Akiva's first level), or it can make itself felt in our standing as a "son" of the Ribono shel Olam, one who, with a Sefer Torah in his arms, marches inward and creates a world all of his own (the combination of R. Akiva's second and third levels).

The murder of either of these two protagonists puts paid to an entire "species." It is an unforgivable act of absolute destruction, and, as the Ribono shel Olam told No'ach, demands the death of the perpetrator in retribution. Still, I imagine that the void left behind by the victim is more dreadfully empty, is more hopelessly and more absolutely in mourning, if he was the Ribono shel Olam's child than if he was not. The two, after all, occupy very different worlds.

We have made a lot of progress but we are not yet home free. Before we can really tell ourselves that we understand the implications of the sixth *Dibra,* we will need to clarify who, in fact, is the aggrieved party when a murder has been committed. It turns out that the answer to this question is not as simple as we would have thought. Our quest will turn out to have been a complicated one. It requires a chapter of its own. Come, we have much to do.

FIFTEEN

The Sixth Dibra *II*

We left off the last chapter wondering who really is the aggrieved party when a murder is committed. I imagine that when you read this closing paragraph you were unable to make much sense of it. It seems fairly obvious that it is the victim who has lost his all. The murderer has clearly sinned against *him*.[1] So, why raise questions that appear as pure pedantry and, in the end, serve only to annoy? Well, I raise it anyway, and you will soon see why.

Here is Ramban to Shemos 20:13.

> **לא תרצח לא תנאף לא תגנב.** אמר, הנה צויתיך להודות שאני בורא את הכל בלב ובמעשה, ולכבד האבות בעבור שהם משתתפים ביצירה, אם כן השמר פן תחבל מעשה ידי ותשפוך דם האדם אשר בראתי לכבודי ולהודות לי בכל אלה . . .
>
> [After the first five *Dibros*, we come to] YOU SHALL NOT MURDER; YOU SHALL NOT COMMIT ADULTERY; YOU SHALL NOT STEAL. This is what the Ribono shel Olam is saying to us [in prohibiting murder]: "Look, I have now commanded you to accept that I am He Who has created everything . . . and also that you are to honor your parents who can lay claim to your respect because they too were partners in your creation. Accordingly, [you will understand that] you must take care not to destroy that which I have created. [Remember that] I brought this person into existence only so that his life might reflect My glory and that he might sing My praises for all that I have done. [If you kill him wantonly, you rob Me of all this.]"

This is a new, and, I imagine, unsuspected dimension to *Lo tirzach*. Victimhood seems to pass from the person who was killed to the Ribono shel Olam.

Let us examine the implications.

Looking back, I see that the wording of the thesis that I have just propounded is, strictly speaking, not accurate; I do not think that the victimhood *passed* to the Ribono shel Olam in the sense that *only* God is viewed as the loser. If you take the time to look at note 1, you will see that the murdered person is still very much in the picture. So let us reword the thesis and suggest that, in Ramban's view, the Ribono shel Olam has joined the actual victim in his victimhood. The murderer is, so to speak, now facing two implacable and unforgiving accusers.[2] (Please read and consider note 2 carefully.)

This Ramban ties in well with the suggestion that we made toward the end of the previous chapter. From the point of view of the Ribono shel Olam, there is surely a difference whether He is a grieving Father Who has lost a son, or whether He is a grieving Monarch Who has lost a subject.

Why did Ramban find it necessary to make the point that the Ribono shel Olam Himself is a victim in every murder? I cannot see any textual awkwardness that would demand such a radical observation. Why was he not satisfied to allow *Lo tirzach* to stand on its own merit—murder is a heinous crime—without the embellishment that identifies the Ribono shel Olam as a victim? I can only explain this on the basis of the theory that I have been suggesting throughout these last few chapters. I think that Ramban was troubled by the question that has been troubling us all along. When is a *mitzvah* more than simply a *mitzvah*? Ramban wonders what it is that lifts murder out of the crowd of rank-and-file *mitzvos* and elevates it to the status of a *Dibra.*

So what is the answer? How does Ramban's discovery of the Ribono shel Olam as victim reveal what it is that grants murder its stature as a *Dibra*? As I read the Ramban, it is that a citizen in a *Mamleches Kohanim VeGoy Kadosh* is more than just an anonymous cipher among the millions who make up a given national entity. He is a *ben yachid,* an only child, of the Ribono shel Olam, an entire species of one (see previous essay) with a value that is beyond reckoning, a uniqueness that makes him irreplaceable. This realization obviously has great importance well beyond the matter of murder. It is not only that, with this awareness lodged firmly in our minds, we will not kill people. Most of us would not do that anyway. But it underlies all our social relationships. Imagine living in a neighborhood in which every single neighbor is a *ben yachid* of the Ribono shel Olam! Some neighbors! Some neighborhood! Welcome to life in a country peopled by a *Mamleches Kohanim VeGoy Kadosh*. The Ribono shel Olam had great things in mind for us when he brought us to Sinai.[3]

There is one little difficulty with which we should deal, before we leave this fascinating topic. The Ramban that we quoted earlier is a part of a long and complex piece in which, among other things, he examines the structure of *Aseres HaDibros*. He suggests that they are to be divided into two sets of five each, the first dealing with *mitzvos* that are to redound to the honor of the Ribono shel Olam, and the second are meant to fill human needs and wants.

Now it seems reasonable to wonder what might be the status of a *Dibra* that is of direct benefit to both the Ribono shel Olam and our fellow man. Take murder as an example. Does it belong in the first group because of the Ribono shel Olam's direct "victimhood" or in the second because it was a person who was killed? The question is, of course, moot because the Ribono shel Olam has made it very clear. It is the sixth *Dibra*, introducing the second group to which the second tablet is devoted.

We face this issue since, as Ramban presents it, the fifth *Dibra*, the obligation to honor our parents, seems to share the duality that we found in connection with the prohibition against murder.

Here, very briefly, are the relevant quotes:

At Shemos 20:12, introducing the fifth *Dibra* (honoring parents) he writes:

הנה השלים כל מה שאנו חייבין בדברי הבורא בעצמו ובכבודו, וחזר לצוות אותנו בעניני הנבראים, והתחיל מן האב שהוא לתולדותיו כענין בורא משתתף ביצירה.

Having finished all that we are obligated toward the Creator Himself and His glory, He turns now to command us about those matters that concern created beings. He begins with the father for, in relation to his offspring, he is akin to a creator, being a partner with Him in the forming of the child.[4]

Now, nothing could be clearer. Kibud Av VaEim concerns "created beings." This is further confirmed by Ramban's next sentence:

כי השם אבינו הראשון, והמוליד אבינו האחרון, ולכך אמר במשנה תורה (דברים ה טז) כאשר צויתיך בכבודי כן אנכי מצוך בכבוד המשתתף עמי ביצירתך.

God is our first[5] father and he who begets us is our last[6] male parent. That is why He said in Devarim, Honor you father and your mother *as I have commanded you.* That is, "Just as I have commanded you concerning My honor, so do I command you concerning the honor of those who have joined Me in your formation."

The meaning appears to be entirely clear. The problem arises later in the Ramban when Ramban divides *Aseres HaDibros* into two groups of five. He writes as follows:

והנה עשרת הדברות חמשה בכבוד הבורא וחמשה לטובת האדם, כי כבד את אביך כבוד האל, כי לכבוד הבורא צוה לכבד האב המשתתף ביצירה, ונשארו חמשה לאדם בצרכו וטובתו.

Thus of *Aseres HaDibros* there are five that refer to the glory of the Creator and five are for the welfare of man. For the fifth *Dibra, Honor your father,* is for the glory of God since it is for the glory of the Creator that He commanded that one honor one's father who is a partner in the formation of the child. [With the decision to list *Kibud Av VaEim* among the first five *Dibros*] we are left with five that are for man's well-being and benefit.

Ramban feels called upon to explain why honoring our parents, a command manifestly directed at humans rather than at the Ribono shel Olam (see the earlier quote concerning the fifth *Dibra*) should have found its way into the first group. His answer seems to be that when we honor our parents we are also honoring the Ribono shel Olam, . . . *since it is for the glory of the Creator that He commanded that one honor one's father who is a partner in the formation of the child.*

Does this not seem to contradict what we learned earlier when we discussed dual victimhood where a murder was committed? There, in spite of the Ribono shel Olam's involvement, the prohibition against murder was deemed to belong among the latter five *Dibros*. Why then should *Kibud Av VaEim* have been placed among the first group of five?

The truth is that this question is a nonstarter. If we read the Ramban carefully we will see that there is no difficulty at all.

It is of course true that in both cases the *Dibra* impacts upon both a human being (respectively, the murder victim and the parents) and the Ribono shel Olam (respectively, the man whom He had formed was destroyed and through the honor paid to the parents honor accrues to Him). However, this shared duality takes radically different forms in the two cases.

Where a murder has been committed the two impacts are parallel but discrete. The loss that accrues to the Ribono shel Olam does not grow out of the loss sustained by the murder victim. The murder victim has lost his life; the Ribono shel Olam has lost a valued servant who, because his personality is unique, can never be replaced. To borrow expressions that have not had a happy history, the two victimizations, though equal, are separate. That determined, the question now arises in which of the two groups into which the *Dibros* are divided should the prohibition against murder be listed? Since we, the recipients of *Aseres HaDibros*, are human, and to humans the human loss is the more immediate, the Ribono shel Olam put murder into the second column.

The relationship between the two honorees in the case of *Kibud Av VaEim* is quite different. The honor that redounds to the Ribono shel Olam when we honor our parents grows out of and is, in fact, a part of the honor that we show our parents. This is so because, as evidenced from the first two passages from the Ramban that we cited above, we are to honor our parents not as an expression of our gratitude for having brought us into this world, but *because* they did what they did in partnership with the Ribono shel Olam. Now clearly if I am to honor someone because he is in partnership with God, that honor itself expresses God's honor.

Viewed thus, it is of course completely logical that *Kibud Av VaEim* be placed in the first group.

We need to add one more thought and then we will be done with this extremely complex section.

I find it fascinating that the Ramban chose to see the rationale for the *mitzvah* of *Kibud Av VaEim* in the partnership that exists between the parents and the Ribono shel Olam, rather than in the need to show parents gratitude for having brought us into the world.

The assumption that the obligation to honor our parents derives from the need to show gratitude to those who have done so much for us has had very wide currency over the centuries. In a random sampling of what is available to me at this moment, I can point to the Sefer HaChinuch and the Chovas HaLevavos (Sha'ar Avodas HaElohim) among the Rishonim, and to Rav Dessler (Michtav MeiEliyahu, vol. 3, p. 95) and my own Rebbi, R. Aryeh Carmel, R. Dessler's great student (*Master Plan,* p. 123) among contemporary thinkers who all espouse this idea. Certainly, if I remember correctly, it was what I was taught as a child.

Why does the Ramban not even consider this option?[7]

Of course there is no way to answer this question with any certitude. However, I suspect that this is one more example where the Ramban is interested in the same question that I have been asking myself in the last few chapters. What is it that qualifies just those *mitzvos* that are a part of *Aseres HaDibros*, as *Dibros*?

It could well be that if it were just a matter of withholding appreciation from parents who so richly deserve our gratitude, that would not qualify this *mitzvah* as a *Dibra*. There are many commands that govern our relationship to our fellows that did not make it to *Aseres HaDibros*.

However, now that Ramban has determined that the basis for honoring our parents is their partnership with the Ribono shel Olam, and that, as we have learned in this chapter, by honoring them we are indeed honoring the Ribono shel Olam, then it is a different story altogether.

The home in a *Mamleches Kohanim VeGoy Kadosh* does indeed become a *Mikdash Me'at,* a mini-Beis HaMikdash, with the Ribono shel Olam, through His surrogate partners, a constant presence.

Be honest with yourselves, dear Readers. Is it not wonderful to be a *Yid*?!

SIXTEEN

The Seventh Dibra

לא תנאף, *Do not commit adultery.*

The seventh *Dibra* forbids intimate relations with another man's wife. It is listed in Sefer HaMitzvos, Negative Commands, 347. Things seem uncomplicated. We know from quotes that I cited in the previous chapter that in Ramban's opinion the second tablet was devoted to the five *Dibros* that are concerned with relationships between man and man. Certainly adultery fits right into this grouping. Few things undermine society's peace and harmony as much as a wife's faithlessness. Everything is evidently as it should be. *Aseres HaDibros* are shaping up exactly as we would have expected.

Still, to be true to the system that we have adopted, we need to discover what it is about adultery that wins this negative *mitzvah* its place among the *Dibros*. Once more, Ramban will be our guide since, against all expectations, he injects a consideration that has nothing at all to do with the havoc that adultery can, and almost always does, cause in people's lives. Here is what he says at Shemos 20:13.

> **ולא תנאף אשת רעך** כי תחבל ענין כבוד האבות לכפור באמת ולהודות בשקר, כי לא ידעו את אביהם ויתנו כבודם לאחר, כאשר יעשו עובדי ע"ז אומרים לעץ אבי אתה.
>
> DO NOT VIOLATE YOUR FELLOW'S WIFE, because if you do, you would undermine the principle of honoring the parents [causing the children] to deny the truth and acknowledge falsehood. They will not know their fathers and will thus show honor to another, just as idol-worshippers do who transfer the obeisance due to the Ribono shel Olam to a wooden image instead. They say to this image, "You are my father!"[1]

Why? Why factor in a seemingly artificial complication when the act of disloyalty itself seems so patently self-sufficient? What Ramban is doing here is eerily reminiscent of what he did in the sixth *Dibra, Lo tirzach.* In both cases he seems bent upon conjuring up an unexpected victim. Earlier it had been the Ribono shel Olam Who had been called into service, and here it is apparently the adulterer. If the illicit union results in a child, this child will think that he is the offspring of his mother's husband and honor him as his father, not knowing that the honor that he is bound to show his father is really due to the man who had violated his mother.[2]

In my opinion, there can be only one explanation. Adultery as a negative *mitzvah* needs no embellishment. As a *Dibra,* unadorned by more fundamental considerations, it would fall short. Ramban is intent upon digging deeper and finding the dimension that could lift this act from a personal tragedy into a constitutional crisis. What underlying quality is there that could move adultery from the particular to the general? What is there about a *Mamleches Kohanim VeGoy Kadosh* that would be mortally wounded by such an egregious act of disloyalty?

In *Aseres HaDibros,* Ramban has discovered the Jewish family as the building block of Klal Yisrael.

In chapter 13 we began to trace the significance of our vertical relationships, those that make us children of our parents and parents of our children. Now that we have learned from the Ramban that *Lo Tin'af* is really an extension of *Kibud Av VaEim,* it is natural that we should continue along the same lines. The concept of Jewish parenthood can use a little more analysis.

Let me share with you the significance that I attach to the wording of the Ramban. Here it is again, in translation: *They will not know their fathers and will thus show honor to another, just as idol worshippers do who transfer the obeisance due to the Ribono shel Olam to a wooden image instead.*

I will give a short general background, which will enable me to make the point that I wish to make.

There are many different forms that the honor that we owe to our parents can be expressed. Rambam, Hilchos Mamrim 6:3, writes as follows:

אי זהו מורא ואי זהו כבוד. מורא לא עומד במקומו ולא יושב במקומו ולא סותר את דבריו ולא מכריע את דבריו ולא יקרא לו בשמו . . . אי זהו כבוד מאכיל ומשקה מלביש ומכסה משל האב ואם אין ממון לאב ויש ממון לבן כופין אותו וזן אביו ואמו כפי מה שהוא יכול ומוציא ומכניס ומשמשו בשאר הדברים שהשמשים משמשים בהן את הרב ועומד מפניו כדרך שהוא עומד מפני רבו.

How does awe express itself and how does honor express itself? Awe expresses itself in that the son will not stand in a place reserved for his father, nor will he sit in his father's place, he will not contradict his father, nor will he voice either agreement or disagreement with what his father says. . . . How does honor express itself? He feeds his father and gives him drink, he clothes him and covers him . . . he takes him out and brings him in and renders him all the help that a servant would do for his master. He stands up in his father's presence just as a servant stands up for his master.

Rambam points out that the respect that a son is bound to show his father is of a kind with the service that a servant must perform for his master. From this we may conclude that the obligation begins with the father's need. The father requires help; the son is obliged to render it. That may seem obvious and I suppose that it is obvious. I mention it only in order to highlight the difference between these forms of honor and the one that I am about to discuss.

Dear Reader! At this point you have to start concentrating. We are about to discover dimensions to the *mitzvah* of *Kibud Av VaEim* that we have never before come across. A new world is about to open for us.[3]

We will quote a part of the Ramban to Shemos 20:12. This small passage is concerned about the fact that the Torah commands us to honor our parents, but apparently gives us no directions concerning the form that our expression of respect ought to take. Ramban will maintain that the essential forms of the respect that are demanded of us are, in fact, clearly stated in the Torah. If we read what the Torah says carefully, we will soon find out what it prescribes for the conscientious son.

This daring assertion is based on something Ramban had said in the paragraph preceding the one that we will now quote. There Ramban asserted that the mitzvah of Kibud Av VaEim is based on our parents' partnership with the Ribono shel Olam in the formation of their children. If you turn back to chapter 15 you will see a short quote from that Ramban where he says that the Ribono shel Olam is our first father, and our biological father is our last father.[4] The point that the Ramban will make in the piece that we are about to quote is that the honor to which the fifth *Dibra* entitles the father consists of precisely those marks of respect that the earlier parts of *Aseres HaDibros* commanded us to show the Ribono shel Olam.

ולא פירש הכתוב הכבוד, שהוא נלמד מן הכבוד הנאמר למעלה באב הראשון יתברך, שיודה בו שהוא אביו, ולא יכפור בו לאמר על אדם אחר שהוא אביו, ולא יעבדנו כבן לירושתו, או לענין אחר שיצפה ממנו, ולא ישא שם אביו וישבע בחיי אביו לשוא ולשקר ויכנסו בכלל הכבוד דברים אחרים, כי בכל כבודו נצטווינו, ומפורשים הם בדברי רבותינו (קדושין לא:).

The Torah had no need to detail the specific actions that would express the respect that we owe our parents, because all that can be learned from what was said earlier concerning the honor due to the Ribono shel Olam Who is our first Father. These standards oblige us to affirm that our biological father is indeed our father (parallel to the first *Dibra* regarding the Ribono shel Olam) and forbids us to call any other person "father" (parallel to the second *Dibra*). They forbid us to serve our father for ulterior motives, for example, because of an anticipated inheritance or some other favor that we might wish to influence (parallel to the words, *to those that love Me* in the second *Dibra* [see Ramban at Shemos 20:6] [Beis HaYayin]). Further, they forbid us to "take our parents' name in vain" in the sense that we may not make a false or frivolous oath, swearing by our father's life (parallel to the third *Dibra*).

In addition to these there are also other services that are required under the rubric of *Kibud Av VaEim*, since the command is broad enough to include all possible expressions of honor. [Here Ramban is referring to the formal services that we encountered in the quote from the Rambam that we cited earlier.]

I said earlier that Ramban is beckoning us to make our entry into a new world. Let me spell out what this means. In the first paragraph above, Ramban lists a series of obligations that we have toward our parents (to affirm their parentage, not to call another person "father," not to serve them for ulterior motives, not to take their name in vain, nor to make false or frivolous oaths by their life) that, to the best of my knowledge, do not appear either in the Gemara or in the Shulchan Aruch. Ramban goes even further. He believes that these "new" categories of showing respect actually reside in the simple meaning of the words, *Honor your father and your mother*. The services of which we spoke earlier, the ones actually mentioned by Chazal and recorded in Rambam and the Shulchan Aruch, are not even included in the Torah's words, but are considered marks of respect only *since the command is broad enough to include all possible expressions of honor.*

Earlier in this essay I made the point that the conventional services that children are called upon to perform for their parents, the ones that are mentioned in the Gemara and codified by the Rambam and the Shulchan Aruch, begin with the father's need. The father requires help; the son is obliged to render it. I would like to suggest that that is not the case in the new category suggested by the Ramban. It seems to me that when the son is obliged to acknowledge his father and not to deny him, together with all the other details that follow these two as Ramban enumerates them, these are not situations in which the parent is lacking something and the children are commanded to supply it. Rather, it seems to me that the obligation begins with the son. It is he who has the need, he who is asked to define himself in relation to his parents. It is he who would cut himself loose from any Jewish anchorage if he thought of his parents disparagingly, he who would set himself hopelessly adrift if carelessly or viciously he would make light of them or their precious names.[5]

It is time now to return to the Ramban that we quoted at the beginning of this essay, the one where he explains the Torah's stand against adultery on the basis that the child who might eventually be born from that union would not know who his biological father is and would therefore not be able to fulfill the demands that the fifth *Dibra, Kibud Av VaEim,* makes upon him. Now, wonder of wonders, the Ramban does not say that, not knowing who his father is, he will not be able to feed him or to clothe him or to render to him all those modes of helpfulness that belong to a servant's duties toward his master. All these he bypasses and mentions only the unconventional duty that Ramban, apparently alone among the standard commentators, reads into the text. The child might call another man "Father"! Why is that?

It seems to me that there is only one possible explanation. There is nothing about the father's loss of his son's service that would qualify adultery as a *Dibra.* There is no doubt that the father loses gravely when his son is not aware of their relationship, but there is also no doubt that that damage does not rank any higher than, let us say, a person's loss of limb through another's negligence. The Torah has much to say about damages and torts but none of these make it into *Aseres HaDibros.* Jewish identity is another matter. We are back to where we were in chapter 13 where we analyzed the Jewish value of the Jewish family in connection with the fifth *Dibra, Kibud Av VaEim.* The Ramban connects the two *Dibros* and indeed it transpires that they both defend the same value that is so basic to a *Mamleches Kohanim VeGoy Kadosh.*

SEVENTEEN

The Eighth Dibra[1]

לא תגנב, *Do not steal.*

At first sight, the eighth *Dibra,* the one that prohibits kidnapping (see Rambam, Negative Commands 243 and 258), seemed to me to be out of place among the ten *Dibros.* Stealing another person is so specialized a crime, is so much a world of its own, that it is hard to see it as a general category under which other evils can or ought to be subsumed. What, I wondered, is so fundamental about the crime of kidnapping that wins it a place among so tiny and select a grouping that only nine others made the grade?

However, I learned soon enough that even a superficial review of the pertinent *halachos* can set us straight. Far from being the interloper that I had judged it to be, kidnapping belongs right in there with all those other *Dibros.* Like them, it too establishes one of the constitutional principles that, together, form the bedrock upon which a *Mamleches Kohanim VeGoy Kadosh* can arise.

We need to do some learning. As we enter into this *sugia* it seems to me that we can safely drop "kidnapping" and move over to "*goneiv nefesh.*" I feel more comfortable with that and, I suspect, so will you. So let us review what the constituent parts of this capital crime are. What must be done if the death penalty is to be incurred?[2]

There are three discrete parts: The perpetrator must "steal" the victim; subsequent to having stolen him, he must have the victim perform some act of servitude; and then he must sell him as a slave. Each of these three elements is carefully defined by the *halachah,* but for the purpose of our analysis we can get by without all the details. However, it *is* necessary to define these three components correctly. That requires a little bit of background. As a first step, we need to get acquainted with what, in *halachah,* constitutes an act of stealing. Again we are heading for only a general definition. It is this: In order for an act to be considered stealing, the thief must perform a *kinyan*, that is, an act that, if he were buying this object legitimately, would result in the full and legal transfer of the object. Theft, then, is also a kind of "acquisition." It is only that since it takes place without the agreement of the owner, the "transfer" stops short of bringing about an actual change of ownership. Its efficacy is limited to bringing about a relationship between the thief and the object that will saddle him with those responsibilities that the *halachah* imposes upon a thief.

So much for the first requirement that postulates that an act of *geneivah* must have taken place.

The second requirement, that the perpetrator must impose some act of service upon the victim, is simple enough. Nothing elaborate is required. Even a minor benefit derived from the victim's body, such as having him stand in front of the perpetrator to act as a screen from the wind, satisfies this requirement.

The third element, that the perpetrator sell the victim into servitude, forces us once more to deal with the issue of valid *kinyanim*. Clearly this third element will not have taken place unless the buyer acquires the victim through a *kinyan* that the *halachah* recognizes as being valid for such a transfer of ownership.

None of this sounds very complicated, does it?

That statement is absolutely true. None of what we have now said *sounds* at all complicated. The problem is only that our presentation of the first and third requirements makes no sense at all. It is all very well to speak of valid *kinyanim* being required both for establishing that a given act can be viewed as a halachically recognized process of stealing, and for a valid sale to have taken place. But an even more fundamental requirement than these two is that the object that is being transferred should be halachically subject to transfer. And that is not the case when we speak of *goneiv nefesh*. A human being, unless he or she is an *eved* or *shifchah Kena'ani[s,]*[3] cannot be stolen and cannot be sold for the very good reason that a human being cannot be owned. We do not own our own bodies; clearly no one else can own us either. One cannot steal a person from himself because he does not own himself.[4] One cannot sell a person to another because one can sell only what one owns and one cannot buy anybody from another because one can buy only what one is able to own.[5]

It turns out that neither the first element, the requirement that the perpetrator *steal* the victim, nor the third element, that he *sell* the victim, partakes of any reality. From beginning to end, the process of *goneiv nefesh* is in the nature of a non-event. It is all done as though with mirrors. In the actual world of the *halachah* nothing really happens—and the perpetrator is done to death! How are we to understand this?

It seems to me that the very unreality of this crime explains the seriousness with which the Torah views it. The crime that the perpetrator commits is one of misreading the very essence of humanity. He treats his fellow *as though he were* an object. He "steals" him as though he could be stolen; he uses him as though it were possible to have the right to use another Jew;[6] he sells him as though he could be sold.

That is the crime of the *goneiv nefesh* and that is what earned it the standing to be included in *Aseres HaDibros*. There can be no more basic requirement for a *Mamleches Kohanim VeGoy Kadosh* than that each human being is recognized, first and foremost, as being human, infinitely and absolutely human. Each and every one of us is a subject, not an object.

Let us learn something about subjects and objects.

Reishis Chochmoh, Sha'ar HaYir'ah has a section in which he cites various Chazal that deal with the process of dying and that record some of the questions that we will be asked once we stand before the Ribono shel Olam's throne to give an accounting of our lives. Here is R. Yosi's tradition concerning those questions. We will be asked:

> כלום עסקת בתורה ובגמילות חסדים והמלכת לקונך שחרית וערבית והמלכת את חברך בנחת רוח?
>
> Did you concern yourself deeply with the study of Torah and the practice of kindness? Did you crown God king every morning and evening? Did you crown your fellows king in a pleasant, nonabrasive manner?

We can leave the first question aside. We know the importance of learning and caring. We can understand the second question, the one concerning *Kri'as Shema*. For those of us who do not always *daven* with the requisite concentration, that question too, though scary, is reasonable. But what about the last question? Did we crown our fellow king? And in exactly the same language as is used in asking us whether we crowned God king? In what sense are we called upon to pronounce other people as "king" over ourselves? And if we are, is he not obliged to pronounce me king over him? So where does that leave us?

It seems to me that we are back with our old friends, objects and subjects. Here is how. We all, by nature, view ourselves as "king" in our own little world. I am at the center of my concerns. I judge all the people with whom I come into contact, all the events that happen around me, from my own point of view. My interest in them is largely limited to the question of how they impact upon me. I may be lecturing in a hall with hundreds of people in the audience. They all play object to my leading role as subject. I am buoyed by their interest, crushed by evidence of their boredom. Their laughter at my poor little jokes brings a lilt to my voice, a song to my heart. If they don't get it, I get it. I am deflated and am hit with the sudden realization that I am no good; my dreams of a useful future lie in ruins and my life is a failure. Believe me, that is how it is. You can make a little allowance for hyperbole, but not much.

My obligation to crown my friend king demands that I recognize him as "king" in his world as much as I am "king" in mine. It forces me to come to grips with the devastating realization that in his world I am a poor and rather uninteresting object to his subject, to the same extent that he plays that role in mine.

It is interesting, is it not, that Chazal demand of me that I crown my friend king, *benachas ru'ach,* which I translated as *in a pleasant, nonabrasive manner*. Abdicating a throne does not come easily. Most of us would feel grumpy and resentful by being suddenly demoted to become another's chattel. But the Ribono shel Olam asks us to be understanding.

We have now discovered that the eighth *Dibra* clearly belongs among *Aseres HaDibros*. It lays the groundwork for the erection of a holy society.

EIGHTEEN

The Ninth Dibra

לא תענה ברעך עד שקר, *Do not bear false witness against your fellow.*

This *Dibra* forbids witnesses to testify falsely in court. It appears in Rambam's Sefer HaMitzvos under Negative Commands 285. Let us now rise to the challenge of working out a possible reason why this *mitzvah* may have been included in *Aseres HaDibros.* Our analysis will take us into a general examination of the judicial function of the *Batei Din* as these are contemplated by the Torah.

There is a cryptic phrase right at the beginning of Sefer Devarim that, as Ramban reads it, can throw important light upon the judiciary and upon the source of its authority and power.

At the beginning of the Sefer, Moshe Rabbeinu describes how, long ago, he decided to appoint judges who would be able to assist him in his judicial duties. It was all too much for a single person to handle. He recalls the charge that he made to the chosen judges. He admonished them to live up to the very high standards that would be required of them.

Devarim 1:17 reads as follows:

> לא תכירו פנים במשפט כקטן כגדל תשמעון לא תגורו מפני איש כי המשפט לאלהים הוא והדבר אשר יקשה מכם תקרבון אלי ושמעתיו.
>
> Do not show favoritism in judgment.
>
> Grant a fair hearing to both the weak and the powerful.
>
> Fear no man, for judgment belongs to God.
>
> Bring any matter that is too difficult for you to me, and I shall listen to it.

We are interested in the third line. What, precisely, is meant by the words . . . *for judgment belongs to God*? Here is what Ramban writes:

> וטעם כי המשפט לאלהים הוא כטעם כי לא לאדם תשפטו כי לה' ועמכם בדבר משפט (דהי"ב יט ו) לומר כי לאלהים לעשות משפט בין יצוריו, כי על

כן בראם, להיות ביניהם יושר וצדק, ולהציל גזול מיד עושקו (ו)נתן אתכם במקומו, ואם תגורו ותעשו חמס הנה חטאתם לה' כי מעלתם בשליחותו.

The words *for justice belongs to God* . . . teach that, since it is God Who created men, it is for Him to execute justice among them, making sure that fairness and justice should prevail and making sure to save the oppressed from his oppressor.[1] [However, since ours is a physical world and the Ribono shel Olam cannot Himself sit in actual judgment] He designated you in His stead. And if you will be afraid and act corruptly . . . you will have betrayed the mission with which He entrusted you.

This is an exciting Ramban. In just a few words he has turned our conception of the nature and workings of the judicial system on its head. Instead of the administration of justice being the Torah's version of "government by the people, for the people", that is, a communal responsibility energized by the need to forestall anarchy, it lies entirely outside the community's normal and undisputed prerogative to fashion and advance its own well-being. Justice, it appears, is a right vested entirely in the Ribono shel Olam Himself. And, while it is true that, in practice, it will be human judges who actually sit in Beis Din, they will function not as the stern arm of society policing its own members, but as representatives of the Ribono shel Olam Who is interested in generating fairness and justice among His often unruly subjects.[2]

At this point we have an expression, A→B. That means that "A" is the cause of "B," where "A" is the fact that the Ribono shel Olam created us and "B" is His "obligation" to undertake the application of justice as a personal responsibility that must be met through the appointment of human Judges who will act in His behalf. We do not, at the moment, have an explanation why this should be so.

I believe that in this short phrase, Ramban touches upon the profoundly significant subject of "individual identity" and "*tzibur* (communal) identity" within the body of Klal Yisrael. We have to spend a little time on this if we are to make it clear.

In an entirely different context, Ramban informs us that

the individual loses his individual significance once he has blended into a *tzibur*. The *tzibur* in *halachah* has much in common with the modern concept of the corporation. The very nature of a corporation is such that it, not the individuals who belong within it, is the legal entity that is the owner of record. It is interesting that in Britain, the famous American Inc. (incorporated) is expressed as Ltd. (limited [liability]). The "Ltd" expresses the idea that any liability that might burden the corporation cannot be collected from the individual participants. If General Motors defaults on a debt, the chairman will not have his private house or car taken. The debtor is not any or all the individuals who own the shares of the company, but the company itself.

Ramban to VaYikra 1:2 teaches this idea in connection with the *semichah,* the "laying on of the hands" upon the animals, that the owner of a *korban* must perform before his sacrifice is slaughtered. He explains that sacrifices fall into two categories: the "individual" and the "communal."[3] An "individual" sacrifice requires *semichah;* a communal sacrifice does not. The difference between the two does not involve the number of owners. An "individual" *korban* may have as many owners as the communal one, as long as these banded together as a partnership and not as a corporation. In a partnership, each of the partners is, as an individual, a part owner, and all the partners, even if they are counted in their thousands, will have to perform an individual *semichah.* In the *korban tzibur* there *is* no individual owner (that is, not even a "part" owner) and no *semichah* at all is required. The corporation (or *tzibur*) is a legal entity that has no existence outside the law.

This is what I meant earlier when I said that in a *tzibur* or corporate entity the individual *as* individual loses his identity.

However, the corporate entity known as "Klal Yisrael" is different. Although Klal Yisrael is certainly a "*tzibur*" (witness the fact that its communal sacrifices do not require *semichah*), the people who make up the Klal are not at all lost in the crowd. Their individuality is sacrosanct even when legally they are functioning in a corporate mode.[4] Ramban (BeMidbar 1:3) affirms this by pointing out that even as they were being counted by means of the half *shekalim* that stood in for them, each one was required to proclaim his name.[5] In this matter they, or rather we, are comparable to the stars. Although the Torah (Bereishis 15:5) proclaims them to be an infinitude,[6] Tehilim (147:4) stresses that the Ribono shel Olam assigns individual names to each of them.[7]

I think that we can now safely return to our original problem. We failed to understand why the fact that the Ribono shel Olam created us made it necessary that only He, rather than a community-developed and delegated Bais Din, could be our true judge. Why was it necessary for the Ramban to relegate all Batei Din into the role of "stand-ins" for the Ribono shel Olam, rather than treating them as functioning courts of law as we understand that term in other contexts?"

I think that it is for the same reason that Klal Yisrael may never be numbered (see note 4). It stems from the refusal to grant the *tzibur* hegemony over the individuals of whom it is comprised. There is simply no concept in the Torah that would allow the *tzibur* to impose its will or its needs upon an individual.[8] He cannot be made to yield to its demands any more than a star in the sky would have to allow itself to be controlled by the aggregate of stars in the firmament. The individualism of the citizen of the *Mamleches Kohanim VeGoy Kadosh* is absolute. God alone can impose His will upon him.

And that is why, in every Beis Din, the Ribono shel Olam is present among the judges.[9] And that is why the ninth *Dibra* belongs among *Aseres HaDibros*. As a witness rises in a Jewish court to testify in favor of one of the litigants and thereby, of course, testifies against the other, he must understand the enormity of what he is undertaking. The Ribono shel Olam is there listening to him, and the Ribono shel Olam is interested in what he has to say. The testimony that he is delivering is leveled against the Ribono shel Olam's only child[10]—it matters to Him a great deal. That is the nature of civil law or, let us say, that is the nature of life, in a *Mamleches Kohanim VeGoy Kadosh*.

NINETEEN

The Tenth Dibra

לא תחמד ..., *Do not covet....*

As we all know, *Aseres HaDibros* appear twice in the Torah, once in Yisro and once in VaEschanan. There are some major and some minor differences between the two versions and much has been written to explain how the two interact with each other. In the tenth *Dibra,* which forbids us to covet what someone else owns, the two versions use different verbs in the all-important opening phrase. Yisro has *Lo tachmod* [your neighbor's house] and VaEschanan has [*Ve*]*Lo tisaveh* [your neighbor's house.] These two expressions are not synonymous and forbid two different aspects of "coveting". When I cast an envious glance at that which my neighbor possesses I begin by craving it. When that feeling becomes strong enough, I will likely lay plans to obtain it. I may decide to ask him to sell it to me and, if he refuses, I may begin to pester him repeatedly. If nothing helps I might draft friends to intercede for me. The initial transgression, when I permit my jealousy to develop into a real craving, is interdicted under the VaEschanan version (Negative Mitzvos 266). "Tisaveh" derives from the root אוה, *to desire.* When I begin to take actions designed to break down the owner's resistance, I transgress the interdiction against *chimud* (from חמד, *to harbor a determination*) to force the owner to accede to my thirst for possession.

Why did just these two prohibitions rise to the level of *Dibros*? It is the same old question that has bothered us with some of the other *Dibros.* There seem to be so many other interpersonal issues—hurtful talk, evil gossip, vengeance, bearing grudges,[1] and the like—that somehow did not make the grade. And let us stress that even stealing, unless it takes the form of kidnapping, also does not figure.

That last example, stealing, is, in a way, the hardest of our problems. I have in mind Rambam's formulation in Geseilah VeAveidah 1:11: *If we permit ourselves to crave, we may readily come to plot and importune. If we plot and importune we may eas-*

ily end up stealing. For if the owner refuses to sell even though we offered him generous payment and even though we arranged for all manner of people to beg him to relent, there is a good chance that, in the end, we will steal the object. Note well: Rambam underlines the seriousness of *ta'avah* and *chimud* by warning that they might lead to stealing, which apparently he views as the more heinous crime. Why then should these two prohibitions, which only feed into the possibility of theft, be *Dibros* while theft itself is not.[2]

In our attempts to understand the first nine *Dibros,* we turned often to the Ramban who, as you will all surely recall, opened many doors for us. We go to him once more, though his treatment of the tenth *Dibra* seems choppy and incomplete. He does not devote even one self-contained comment to it. He mentions it obliquely, almost coincidentally, while his concerns are with other issues. I will quote the three seemingly minor remarks that he makes and then try to make some sense of it all.

Our first stop will be the Ramban on the sixth, seventh, and eighth *Dibros* (Shemos 20:13–14). We have discussed this very difficult Ramban extensively in chapters 15 and 16. However, there is a section toward the end of this piece upon which we have not yet touched. We will now concentrate on that section.

The part of the Ramban that concerns us deals with the sequence in which the *Dibros* are listed. The following sentence occurs: "After that we come to kidnapping, false testimony, and robbery." We have discussed Ramban's use of the term "robbery" to describe *Lo tachmod* in note 2. Here we are interested in Ramban's next sentence: *He that does not covet will never damage another.* What is Ramban saying here? Beis HaYayin suggests, and I believe that this explanation fits better than some alternatives, that this is meant to explain why *Lo tachmod* follows upon murder, violation of another's wife, kidnapping, and testifying falsely. It is meant as a corrective for the preceding *Dibros. Lo tachmod* is to be an antidote for one who has the propensity to damage another.

The concept that someone who refrains from importuning

his friend will also be careful not to cause him any damage certainly requires clarification. However, for the moment, I would like to leave Ramban's reasoning to the side. I am more interested in the fact that Ramban seems to require an explanation for the fact that *Lo tachmod* occupies the place that it does. What is the question to which he appears to be giving an answer? Is he disturbed by the fact that *chimud* rises to the level of a *Dibra* altogether, or is it just its having been selected as the tenth, final *Dibra* that disturbs him? Whichever of the two is the truth, and I would not know how to decide, it seems clear that somehow, in Ramban's mind, *Lo tachmod* seems to require justifications that the other *Dibros* do not. Why?

Here is how Ramban continues from the point at which we just left off.

> והנה השלים כל מה שאדם חייב בשל חברו ואחר כן יבאר המשפטים בפרט, כי המתחייב לחבירו במשפט מן המשפטים אם לא יחמוד ולא יתאוה למה שאינו שלו ישלם מה שעליו.
>
> At this point, all obligations between man and his fellow have been completed, and it is now time to move forward to learn Mishpatim, the part of the Torah that deals with civil law. This is so because civil law often requires that a guilty party will have to pay the person whom he has damaged. Only people who have learned not to covet, nor even to crave, that which does not belong to them, will willingly pay whatever the law might oblige them to pay.

Once more, Ramban seems to feel the need to assign a purpose to *Lo tachmod* that lies outside the *Dibra* itself. Where earlier he described it as capping the four *Dibros* that preceded it, he now defines it as a bridge to *parashas* Mishpatim that follows it. Why not deal with the *Dibra* in its own terms? Why not, for example, share Ibn Ezra's perplexity at a prohibition that seems directed at feelings that need to be controlled rather than at actions that need to be avoided. What is there about this *Dibra* that makes it so different from all the others?

There is a third Ramban, this one at the beginning of

Mishpatim. There he maintains that Mishpatim is to be viewed as an extension of *Lo tachmod.* He writes: *"VeEileh HaMishpatim" has the task of augmenting* LO TACHMOD *for, were a person ignorant of how the law disposes of the ownership of houses and fields and all other kinds of property, he might err by thinking that he has a claim to it and therefore covet it and take it for himself. It is for this reason that the Torah writes,* YOU SHALL PLACE BEFORE THEM *equitable laws which people would gladly accept as arbiter for their relationships and will therefore not covet that to which the law gives them no claim. This truth is taught by the Midrash:* THE WHOLE TORAH DEPENDS UPON EQUITABLE INTERPERSONAL LAWS AND IT IS FOR THIS REASON THAT THE TORAH WRITES MISHPATIM IMMEDIATELY AFTER *Aseres HaDibros.*

How are we to understand these three Rambans?

Upon reflection it seems to me that the entire premise of my questioning has been incorrect. I had assumed that *Lo tachmod,* in its own right, was somehow inferior to the other nine *Dibros* and that this inferiority caused the Ramban to find significance for this *Dibra* in its relationships to other sections rather than in its own character. I was wrong. We will soon see that within its own character it is perhaps the most significant of the *Dibros.* The Ramban has not dealt with the nature of the prohibition because he considers it self-evident for reasons that we will soon spell out. Instead, he focuses upon the relationship between this *Dibra* to what precedes and follows it, because the positioning of this *Dibra* is itself a defining element in this, the pinnacle[3] of *Aseres HaDibros.*

Here is my thesis. I am going to suggest that the last *Dibra,* by being positioned as the last *Dibra,* carries the same weight and the same moment as the first carries by being first. The first *Dibra* is special because all else flows from its premises; the last *Dibra* is equally special because, within it, those premises are encapsulated and actualized. We might say that while the first *Dibra* introduced the Ribono shel Olam to us, the last *Dibra* introduces us to ourselves. In its majestic simplicity it limns the contours of the *Mamleches Kohanim VeGoy Kadosh.*

Let us state our thesis clearly and unambiguously. The hallmark of the citizen-in-good-standing of a *Mamleches Kohanim VeGoy Kadosh* is his self-sufficiency in all matters pertaining to the physical, the this-worldly. He does not notice what his neighbor owns because it is of no interest to him. If somehow it came to his attention it would not occur to him that it might be nice if that object were his. In Ibn Ezra's felicitous metaphor, he is no more stimulated to grouse that he lacks what his neighbor owns, than he would be jealous of a bird's wings. In modern parlance we would say that neither even shows up on his screen.

"Do not covet," the tenth *Dibra* calls out to us, "because if you have internalized the earlier *Dibros* you will know that coveting is so much wasted energy and makes no sense at all. Think for a moment who you are. Do you recall your singularity (*Dibros* 6 and 9)? You are an only child. Would your Father begrudge you a trinket that you really need? What are the values that count in your life (*Dibra* 2)? Are you sure that what you want so badly does not fit into one of Avraham Avinu's four hundred chapters of Avodah Zarah? Have you forgotten your role as a link in the Mesorah (*Dibros* 5, 7, and 8)? Did your father teach you? Are you eager to pass on to your son your craving for a stupid donkey or, God forbid, your neighbor's wife?"

"*Es passt nisht,*"[4] the tenth and last *Dibra* whispers to us. As a citizen in a *Mamleches Kohanim,* you can take your pick between Rashi and the Ramban.[5] If you prefer Rashi that *Kohein* in this context means an *aristocrat,* remember that *noblesse oblige,*[6] nobility imposes responsibility. In high society people do not lick their fingers after a meal. If Ramban's interpretation as *servant* lies closer to your heart, ask yourself whether your Master would withhold from you the tools that you need to do the job. Only Pharaoh was foolish enough to make us find our own straw. If you hire a lady to clean your house, you hand her a mop. And if you do not give her a squeegee she will know that, today, there is no need to clean the windows.

Earlier I asked a question. I believe that we are now equipped to suggest an answer. I wondered why *chimud* makes the grade to become a *Dibra,* whereas stealing, apparently the more heinous crime, does not (see note 2). Perhaps the explanation is as follows: We are all human and occasionally may do things on the spur of the moment that we will later regret. We may steal without having given the matter much thought. We will have done something wicked and foolish, but that does not reveal us as being grounded by seriously leaden feet. *Chimud* is different. It takes time for first the attraction, then the desire, then the craving to build up. After that comes the first diffident request to the owner, then a more insistent needling, then perhaps a more aggressive importuning. There is plenty of time to come to one's senses. When that does not happen, that points to a very profound failing. Your preoccupation with sheer stupidity shows that, to use the latest cool expression, you just don't get it; there is simply nobody at home.

I have a suggestion to make. I think that I can explain why Ramban seems to go out of his way to present *Lo tachmod* as a *Dibra* that acts as a bridge to other sections of the Torah rather than being significant in its own right. Let us remember that first he writes that it is a fitting capping to the four *Dibros* that speak of *refraining* from harming one's fellow, since one who does not covet will certainly not want to do any harm.[7] Then he wrote that it is an appropriate introduction to Mishpatim since one who does not covet will be conscientious about paying for damage that he might, under the laws that Mishpatim legislates, do to his fellow. And lastly he remarks that Mishpatim needed to follow *Lo tachmod* in order to clarify what belongs to whom. Only if Reuven knows that the *halachah* grants the disputed object to Shimon, will he know that he is not permitted to covet it.

Why the insistence that this *Dibra*'s relationships must be examined? None of the other *Dibros* underwent such an examination. So why subject *Lo tachmod* to this treatment?

The answer lies in every line that we have written in this book. *Aseres HaDibros* define the underpinnings of Judaism and the tenth *Dibra* projects the ideal product of this system. He who has worked out how to live with *lo tachmod* will be able to act as a goodwill ambassador to the rest of the Torah. Are we bidden never to harm our neighbor (*Dibros* 6,

7, 8, and 9)? He makes the extra care that we must exercise, palatable. Ownership, he teaches us, is not the outcome of happenstance. We have, we were given, what we need, not more and not less. Let us not play fast and loose with what our neighbor possesses. He too has what he needs and only what he needs. Let us not, by uncaring carelessness, deny him what God so lovingly granted him. A *Mamleches Kohanim VeGoy Kadosh* is a society that is built upon respect. There is no sweeter life than one in which I know that my neighbor will respect my uniqueness even as I respect his.

Am I resentful when, on the basis of the Mishpatim legislation, I have to pay damages to my neighbor? It is true that my mind balks at many of the laws that seem to fly in the face of reasonable expectations.[8] Why may I not charge moderate interest for the loans that I make? Why must my neighbor's lost object be allowed to play havoc with my otherwise orderly life? By what standard of justice should I be obliged to give my Jewish servant the largest slice of pizza? And so on and on and on. *Lo tachmod* will help us over these humps. If I have internalized the lessons of *Lo tachmod*, if I live as a citizen in good standing of a *Mamleches Kohanim VeGoy Kadosh*, my pride in being who I am, in being part of a society of aristocrats, will still all these misgivings. *Es iz gut tzu sein a Yid.*

And, finally, we understand the last Ramban, the one that claimed that *Lo tachmod* requires Mishpatim to define the areas in which *chimud* is forbidden. It is all a part of what we have just learned. Instinct will not serve us here. There are so many laws in Mishpatim that seem to run counter to what ordinary humans would have supposed. Mishpatim is the textbook the task of which is to teach us how a *Mamleches Kohanim VeGoy Kadosh* is expected to live. It is an indispensable instruction manual. Once we have oriented ourselves to living in this brave new world, we are ready for the task of living as God's *segulah*.

TWENTY

Parashas Mishpatim *and the* Eved Ivri

We are nearing the end of the book and it is time to begin pulling together all the threads that we have spun in the earlier chapters. I hope that you will like the pattern that emerges as much as I do.

Here is something to think about. In our *davening* we refer to Shavuos as the *Zeman Matan Toraseinu,*[1] the time when "our" Torah was given. Has it ever struck you what a strange expression "Toraseinu" is?[2] Throughout TaNaCh we have the Torah called *Toras HaShem* or *Toras Elokim;* we even have *Toras Moshe.*[3] But never once is there a reference to *Toras Yisrael.* So in what sense is the Torah "our" Torah?

How are we to understand "*Zeman Matan Toraseinu*"? I feel rather diffident about the suggestion that I am going to make. I suspect that not many people have ever thought along the same lines. I further suspect that not many of you will be willing to give it credence. Still, I offer it for your consideration. Nobody need accept it as objective truth.

Here is my suggestion: The word "Torah" is used in Chumash not only to describe the five books of the Chumash, but also to describe any body of law that is custom-designed for a particular halachic category. Thus we have, *These are the laws* (TORAHS) *governing the* NAZIR (BeMidbar 6:21),[4] or *the* YOLEDES (VaYikra 12:7) and many more. Now, we will devote a significant part of this chapter to the simple proposition that the civil laws that are to govern relationships within the Jewish people will necessarily be very different and more demanding than those that govern other societies. Clearly a nation that looks upon itself as a *Mamleches Kohanim VeGoy Kadosh* will be held to higher standards than are other people. Perhaps then we could translate *Zeman Matan Toraseinu* as *the time that we were given the set of laws that fit* OUR *exalted status, that were custom made for the Ribono shel Olam's* SEGULAH. Taken thus, the expression "our Torah" would be unproblematic. We celebrate Shavuos as the day upon which the Ribono shel Olam introduced us to the kind of society that we would be expected to build if we were to live up to the *segulah* status that the Ribono shel Olam had now conferred upon us.

This, for better or worse, is my suggestion.

Bear with me for the moment. I know that these ideas are not at all the ones with which we have been brought up. Still, if you can live with them at least temporarily, I can promise you a new and challenging experience in studying *parashas* Mishpatim. There will be time enough to commit or to reject by the time you reach the end of this chapter.

The positioning of *parashas* Mishpatim is no simple matter. We expect to find long halachic passages in VaYikra and Devarim, because those two books are clearly devoted to *halachah*. If the laws that are given in Mishpatim had been taught, let us say, intertwined with Kedoshim in VaYikra or Ki Seitzeih in Devarim, it would have occasioned no surprise. However, Shemos, with the one exception of *parshas* Mishpatim, is a narrative book. Its subject matter runs from Yetzi'as Mitzrayim till the raising of the Mishkan. If we could spirit away the one hundred verses that comprise the halachic parts of Mishpatim, that narrative would be seamless and logical. From the narrative standpoint those hundred verses are a disturbing intrusion. Why are they here?[5]

The answer must of course be that Mishpatim is, in fact, a part of the narrative. The story would not have been complete or coherent had it not mentioned that *as part of* MA'AMAD HAR SINAI the Ribono shel Olam gave us *parashas* Mishpatim.

This will require some explaining. It will make this chapter longer than I had planned, but we are going to have to live with that. This is just too important to leave out. In a way the conclusions toward which I have been structuring the entire book will find confirmation in what we are about to learn.

The first Rashi in *parashas* Mishpatim reflects upon the conjunctive *vav* with which *parashas* Mishpatim begins: not *These are the laws* but AND *these are the laws.*[6] Rashi explains that whereas "These" without the *vav* would imply a new beginning, disconnecting that which is to follow from that which came before, "*And* these" implies a continuity. Rashi expresses that continuity by saying, "Just as the earlier laws were given at Sinai, so, too, that which is to follow was given at Sinai." Our task will be to define what precisely is implied by saying that Mishpatim was given at Sinai.

The precise meaning of "given at Sinai" is the subject of a controversy between Mizrachi and Maharal. We will be following Maharal, but, in passing, it is worthwhile to note the length to which Mizrachi is willing to go. He maintains that the phrase conveys the idea that just as *Aseres HaDibros* were given against the background of thunderclaps, so, too, was *parashas* Mishpatim. That is a perception with highly significant repercussions. It actually raises *parashas* Mishpatim to a level approaching that of the *Aseres HaDibros.*

Maharal (Gur Aryeh) is unwilling to go so far. He cites proof-texts that indicate that the thunderclaps were associated exclusively with *Aseres HaDibros.* His understanding of the concept "given at Sinai" is as follows. He begins by noting that, in our tradition, *all* the *mitzvos* in the Torah were given three times: once at Sinai, once from the Ohel Mo'ed during our travels through the desert, and once more in Arvos Moav, the east bank of the Yarden (Chagigah 6b and elsewhere).[7] That given, Maharal wonders what Rashi means when he says that the conjunction at the start of Mishpatim teaches us that just as *Aseres HaDibros* were given at Sinai, so too was Mishpatim given at Sinai. Since *all* the *mitzvos* were given there, what is special about Mishpatim?

Here is Maharal's explanation. He begins by attempting to understand why indeed all the *mitzvos* had to be given three times at three different locations. He posits that there are certain clusters of *mitzvos* that, by their very nature, belonged to one of those three locations. For example, *Aseres HaDibros* "belong" to Sinai; the laws of the sacrificial service "belong" to the Ohel Mo'ed, and—let us pick our own example—the laws of war and conquest "belong" to Arvos Moav as we stood at the very border of Eretz Yisrael, ready to move in. "All" the *mitzvos* were given in each of these locations because the Ribono shel Olam does not want to split the totality of the *TaRYaG*

Mitzvos into radically different categories. Among them there are certainly different groupings, but essentially they always belong together. Therefore, since certain *mitzvos* had to be given at Sinai, the other *mitzvos* concerning which there was no such need were still given together with them. The same is of course true for the other two locations.

It transpires that at each of the three locations there were those *mitzvos* that were indigenous to it and there were others that had no particular affinity to that place but were nevertheless given there in order to preserve the essential unity among the *TaRYaG Mitzvos.*

When Chazal affirm that the *vav* of *ve'eileh* teaches that there is a similarity between the *Aseres HaDibros* and Mishpatim in that they were both "given at Sinai," they mean that just as the former *belong* to Sinai indigenously, so too does *parashas* Mishpatim. Mishpatim was told to Moshe Rabbeinu together with *Aseres HaDibros* because *Ma'amad Har Sinai* would have been incomplete had Mishpatim not been given at the same time.

Clearly, the difference between Mizrachi and Maharal is one of degree only. Both agree that *Aseres HaDibros* and Mishpatim are inseparable. It is up to us to work out why this should be so.

Maharal does not explain why Mishpatim *belongs* to Sinai more than any other *mitzvos.* Here is what I think. We have now learned that, just as there is a *Toras HaNazir* and a *Toras HaYoledes* there is also a *Toras Yisrael.* It stands to reason, does it not? If we are to be a *segulah* to the Ribono shel Olam, if we are to take our place among the nations as a *Mamleches Kohanim VeGoy Kadosh,* it follows that the laws and norms that contour our lives and peoplehood would be different from those that are appropriate to people who define themselves or are defined by others in different terms with different aspirations.

How are differences best displayed? The late, great Rav Hutner answered that the more similar two units are to each other, the more boldly is the one factor that differentiates between them accented. Yaakov and Eisav were twins. The two goats that stood at the center of the Yom Kippur service in the Beis HaMikdash, one destined to "carry" Israel's sins to the mountains, the other to be sacrificed in the Beis HaMikdash, had to be otherwise as close to identical as possible. We can borrow this idea for our own purposes. If we were to illustrate our differences from the other nations by the fact that we shake the *Lulav* and they do not, that would show very little. Ours is a different religion from theirs, our history is a different history, our dreams are different dreams. We express ourselves in different idioms. But if the underlying premises of our *civil* law differ from theirs in spite of the fact that the need that such laws are designed to fill—protecting society from anarchy—is common to all of us, then indeed it becomes evident that our singularity rests on foundations that run very, very deep.

Ma'amad Har Sinai made us into a *Mamleches Kohanim VeGoy Kadosh. Aseres HaDibros* laid down the constitutional framework upon which such a nation would flourish. Mishpatim welcomes us to contemplate the implications of the civil law that would define relationships and obligations within such a society. Without Mishpatim as a part of *Ma'amad Har Sinai*, we would not have had any idea what it would mean for us to become a *Mamleches Kohanim VeGoy Kadosh*. We might say that Mishpatim is the "Rashi" on that phrase.

I had wanted to complete this book by illustrating from a number of the Mishpatim *halachos* just how the standards that are demanded of us—the *Mamleches Kohanim VeGoy Kadosh*—are immeasurably higher than those demanded of other societies. However, the book is already longer than it should be, and I am going to have to leave that plan aside. The fact is that my idea about the function of *parashas* Mishpatim has been incubating in my mind for a couple of years and I have already dealt with it two years ago in my *Ramban as Guide to Today's Perplexed*. In the Epilogue to that book I discussed a number of *mitzvos* such as returning lost objects, forgiving debts at the end of the Shemitah year, and the like. If you have the book and want to reread that Epilogue at this point, I believe that you would not regret it. Here, I will concentrate on just one *mitzvah,* the one with which Mishpatim begins, the laws governing the *eved Ivri,* the Jewish slave.

THE EVED IVRI

Long before I ever had an opinion about what the nature of Mishpatim might be, I wondered why pride of place, at the beginning of all the laws, should have been awarded to the *eved Ivri.* Of all the issues with which Mishpatim deals, this one seems, in practical terms, to be particularly remote. The possibility of buying an *eved Ivri* is limited to Eretz Yisrael and that only when the majority of Klal Yisrael is living there (Kiddushin 69a). Such conditions still lay far in the future.[8] Moreover, the *eved Ivri* discussed in Mishpatim[9] is a robber who, unable to satisfy the victim's claim for compensation, was sold by the courts in order to raise the necessary funds (see Rashi to Shemos 21:2). It seems highly unlikely that such a situation would arise while we were wandering in the desert. With food and drink coming as gifts from heaven, with the *Anenei Kavod* taking care of the laundry, it seems unlikely that people would be moved to steal from one another.

So, why begin with *eved Ivri*?

The institution of *eved Ivri* is one that to American sensibilities (perhaps too, our own) seems crude and primitive. To sell a person into slavery in order to pay off a debt!? How dreadful and barbaric! So much for American sensibilities! The fact is, of course, that it projects exquisite sensitivity and, when we think about it, evidences the love and concern that the Ribono shel Olam has for even His erring sons.

Let us quickly rehearse some of the salient features of this institution. In the first place, the sale must take place in private. It is forbidden to sell the thief in the slave market or to stand him up on a platform to show off his advantages to best effect. Once he is bought, the first thing that the new master learns is that for the next six years he will have to feed and clothe the family of his new *eved.* No matter how many children the *eved* has, they all now become the master's responsibility.

The work that the master can demand from his *eved* is strictly limited to activities that will not offend against his dignity. "Slave work" is strictly forbidden. For example, even something as seemingly innocent as having the *eved* carry the master's clothes to the bathhouse is out of bounds.

Then, of course, there is the well-known requirement, . . . *for it is good for him* WITH YOU (Devarim 15:16), from which verse *Tosafos* to Kidushin 20a deduces that if there is only one bed, the master must leave it to the *eved* and make do as best as he can on the floor. This, because whatever the master has that can be described as "good" must be shared "with" the *eved*. Since if the master were to use the bed, the servant would not be "with" him, willy-nilly he must leave it to the *eved*.

So what is actually accomplished by selling the thief? A great deal. He is given an opportunity to live a responsible life as part of a decent family, at peace with himself because he knows that his own wife and children are being fed and clothed by his master. It is true that he will have to work hard, but even that onerous burden will be softened by the knowledge that he will never be asked to compromise his dignity as a human being. In many ways he will be treated as a favored guest. His own comfort will be assured at least at the same level as that which is enjoyed by his master. Six years of living in such non-threatening circumstances will provide a pleasant background against which he will slowly but surely learn that it is possible to live well and satisfyingly without resorting to crime.

Compare that to the brutalizing prison experience in what, nowadays, is euphemistically described as a House of Corrections. Unsurprisingly, the Ribono shel Olam knows something that today's sociologists of crime do not. Rehabilitation *can* be accomplished. It just has to be done right.

Beautiful! Is it not? And yet, suddenly without warning, this heartwarming picture comes crashing down all around us. Our idyllic picture explodes in our faces and we are crushed and broken by what the Torah prescribes for this *eved*. His owner has the right to make him cohabit[10] with a non-Jewish[11] slave girl, in order that children born of that union will, by halachic fiat, be slaves to the owner. Jewish men are forbidden to cohabit with such women, Jewish women are forbidden to cohabit with men who have the same status. And here we have this *eved* forced to do what in other circumstances would have been strictly interdicted for him. We are telling him, "Your Jewishness is somehow tainted. What for others is unthinkable, for you is not only permitted but obligatory. When you stole, you traded in some of your *yiddishkeit*. Go where they are sending you. Spend your nights with the real slaves. Till your years of servitude are up, that is where you belong!"

Can there be a greater horror? Can there be a greater shame?

So how do we bridge this chasm? On the one hand, we have the gentle touch of deep, deep caring; on the other, the unflinching willingness to let truth point where it will. On the one hand, the Ribono shel Olam sees a needy human whose craving for dignity must be honored; on the other, damaged goods, no longer, at least for the present, imbued with the degree of sanctity that would make a liaison with a non-Jewish slave girl unimaginable.

How does the Torah want this hapless *eved Ivri* to view himself? It is true that he had sinned; he had stolen. However, he is willing to make restitution. It is just that he lacks the wherewithal to do what he must. So he was sold. It is what the *halachah* demands; in our vernacular we would say that he has paid his debt to society. What does all this have to do with his Judaism? "Why, dear God, must I be thrown together with a woman with whom I have not a single value in common? I put on my tefillin in the morning and shudder at the memory of the night that went before. I open my Gemara, and feel like a filthy intruder, offensive and disgusting in the eyes of the Tana'im and Amora'im whose words were once my joy and have now become hate-lined daggers to my heart. Why this of all things, O God. Why this?"

And here, dear Readers, I believe that we have the answer to the question that plagued us earlier. We wondered why, of all the *Halachos* in Mishpatim, just the *eved Ivri* was placed first.

Now we know, or at least I think that *I* know. It is because just in this *parshah* we have humanity and Judaism juxtaposed with absolute clarity—and the difference between them is shattering. Let us spell it out. On the one hand, the *eved* is treated with exemplary sensitivity. Lovingly and carefully his path is smoothed at every step; his dignity is coddled with exquisite sensitivity. Can we doubt that this, and only this, is a guaranteed road to healthy rehabilitation? What is the message that we are sending him by means of this considerate treatment? It is this: "As a human being, you have erred badly. You have sinned; you have stolen. But, withal you are still a precious human being. Come, we will take you by the hand and help you to a fresh start."

However, when we look upon this thief as a Jew, it is a different story altogether. It is not so much that he has sinned as that he has failed himself, failed utterly and dismally, to even begin to understand who he is, what life promises him, and what it demands of him.[12] All those fundamental lessons that we have struggled so hard in chapters 9 to 19 to discover in *Aseres HaDibros* have passed him by. For all that he cares, *Ma'amad Har Sinai* might as well not have happened. He is, or at least has become, as close as one can get to such a dreadful pass, an "ethnic" Jew. He has traded in his *Kedushas Yisrael* for a mess of pottage. "Go, lie with a slave girl," we say to him. "It is where you now belong. You owe work to your master. Why let the nights go to waste?"[13]

What a dreadful message to place alongside the other one, which is so rich in patience and understanding.

What, at the end of the day, was so dreadful in what he did? How does he deserve such harsh stricture? He did not eat on Yom Kippur, nor did he desecrate the Shabbos or transgress any of those *mitzvos* by which we tend to define our Judaism. He did none of these; he stole. But wait a moment. That is not a "Jewish" but a human transgression. There is not a nation in the world, living under the rule of law, that does not forbid stealing. To interdict thievery one does not have to be a *Mamleches Kohanim VeGoy Kadosh*. As the old advertisement used to say, "You don't have to be Jewish to enjoy Levi's rye." You don't have to be Jewish to understand that stealing is disallowed.

And yet it is not so. By placing the *parshah* of *eved Ivri* at the very beginning of Mishpatim, the Torah is sending us a very fundamental message. The true test of whether or not you are living up to the standards of a *Mamleches Kohanim VeGoy Kadosh* will be in your civil, not your so-called religious, behavior. It is particularly in those many *mitzvos* that can, in a general way, be subsumed under *Lo tachmod,* that you sanctity will be validated.

This last paragraph, so it seems to me, can serve as the summation of all that I have written in this book. *Ma'amad Har Sinai* was the moment at which the Ribono shel Olam was ready to send history on its path. ואביא אתכם אלי, *And I brought you unto Me.* The covenant that He had forged with the Avos could now be consummated. *Beis Yaakov* and *Benei Yisrael* would light the way back to Him for all to follow.

TWENTY-ONE

Some Answers to Some Significant Questions

Do you remember how we started this book? It was a reasonable enough question. In the Introduction we wondered why, when we have so many *mitzvos* designed to remind us of our redemption from Egypt, there were none at all dedicated to the memory of *Ma'amad Har Sinai.* When we asked that question, all we had in front of us were blank pages, daring us to set out on a path of discovery. What do you think, dear Reader? Are we ready to hazard a guess?

I think I know the answer, or, if not *the* answer, at least *an* answer. *Yetzi'as Mitzrayim* was an event in Jewish history. As Ramban teaches us in his famous comments at the end of Bo (Shemos 13:16), it is certainly the most significant event, since it provides the basis for all our *ikrei emunah.* But, in spite of its profound significance, it is no more than an event. It deserves to be remembered, it must be remembered, but for all that it is no more than an event. Not so *Ma'amad Har Sinai,* as the Ramban in whose footsteps we have walked in these many chapters teaches us. It is not an event in our history but the very stuff of which we and our history are made. There is not a second in our lives in which, if we are thinking Jews, we do not remember it. Husbands and wives need no artificial ceremonies to keep the awareness of their marriage alive for them. They live constantly and consciously within that all-encompassing truth. *Mitzvos* to remind us of *Ma'amad Har Sinai* would be a travesty.

This is the background against which we need to approach one of the questions that we left unanswered in chapter 1. Now would be a good time to reread that chapter and do some thinking on your own. Try your hand at the issues that we introduced there and then let us compare notes. There are of course no exact answers. There will certainly be more than one way of looking at things.

Here is one of the questions that I asked there. *I would like to understand why we, the Jewish people, are divided into* BEIS

YAAKOV *and* BENEI YISRAEL. We had demonstrated that the well-known division, *Beis Yaakov* = Women, *Benei Yisrael* = Men, is probably true only at the level of *d'rash* but that at the level of *p'shat* there must be another meaning.

Here are my thoughts, beginning with just a few words of background. The Jewish people are most immediately considered to be Yaakov's family, rather than that of Avraham and Yitzchak. The expressions *Beis Yaakov* and *Beis Yisrael* occur frequently throughout TaNaCh; *Beis Avraham* and *Beis Yitzchak* are never used to describe the Jewish people.

Now who is this third Patriarch? Is he Yaakov or Yisrael? Berachos 13a makes clear that although after Avram's name was changed to Avraham, it was forbidden to use the old name, this was not the case with the change from Yaakov to Yisrael. Yaakov was still a legitimate name by which to identify this Av, but it would henceforth be *tafel,* subsidiary, to the main name, Yisrael. So he is both; most particularly Yisrael, but also, where demanded by context, Yaakov.

An analysis of the range of implications carried by each name is utterly beyond me. For that, one has to know the entire Torah and have a clear understanding of each passage in which either or both these names occur. It is a complicated issue, one that I will be careful to avoid.

I have a much more modest agenda. I will propose a meaning for the usage as it appears at Shemos 19:3, the verse about which we are currently thinking. It seems logical in terms of both language and context. Even this very narrow submission is made diffidently, as no more than a possibility that resonates with me. I make no claim to objective truth.

I can think of two references in our Siddur in which Yaakov is mentioned together with the other two Avos and is still differentiated from them in that those are looked upon more as individuals, whereas Yaakov/Yisrael is projected as father of a nation. The first is in our daily Shacharis where we read, *But we are . . . the children of Avraham . . . the seed of Yitzchak . . . the* CONGREGATION *of Yaakov. . . .* The other occurs in our Shabbos *minchah* where we have, *Avraham will rejoice; Yitzchak will jubilate; Yaakov* AND HIS SONS *will rest on it.*

There may be more, but I think that these two will suffice to illustrate my point.

It is interesting that, in both these instances, Yaakov rather than Yisrael is used. I suppose that, when we really think about it, this seems logical enough. After all, it was as Yaakov, not as Yisrael, a name given to him much later, that he bore the Shevatim.[1] Once we understand this, it seems natural that when we think about the third Patriarch as father of a nation, "Yaakov" rather than "Yisrael" should be used.[2]

Let us take this line of reasoning a little further. Let us reflect upon the circumstances under which Yaakov received the additional name "Yisrael." He had taken his entire family across the Yabok and then decided to return without them to the bank from which he had come. There he remained *levado,* alone (Bereishis 22:34). It was there, unencumbered by wives or children, that he was given the name Yisrael. Surely the implication is that Yaakov, the man who was defined as *the* main father of a nation, was still able to detach himself from that condition and assert his individuality by seeking out a "*levado*" state for himself. It was specifically in that state that he earned the name Yisrael. "Yisrael" stands for the individual who, while fully absorbed by his people, has nevertheless maintained a separate identity.

And so we begin to understand why "Yisrael" became the main name while Yaakov became the *tafel,* the subsidiary name. It is because in our consciousness we are always individuals before we are members of a group. I "am" before I "belong." It is as simple as that.

When we first raised this issue in chapter 1, we wondered why the Yaakov/Yisrael divide should be so fundamental that at crucial points in our history we are defined specifically as a people made up from both strands. If our interpretation is correct, it would go far toward explaining this phenomenon. The fact that each of us has two identities, that of an individual and that of being a part of the *tzibur* of Klal Yisrael, is too well known and is too pervasive in our lives to require much elucidation. We can get by with a minimum by just reminding ourselves how we make this point at least three times every day when we stand before the Ribono shel Olam in prayer. The entire *Tefillah* is couched in the plural form because, ideally, it is to be prayed *betzibur*, and nevertheless, when we are done, custom has granted us an entire paragraph,[3] couched in the singular, in order to be able to approach the Ribono shel Olam in the individual mode, stressing our personal needs, celebrating our personal relationship.[4] The duality of our Jewish personality requires no complex proof. It is an everyday facet of our lives.

We are ready to get back to Shemos 19:3, the introduction to *Ma'amad Har Sinai*. Moshe Rabbeinu is commanded to address both *Beis Yaakov* and *Benei Yisrael*. Everything falls logically into place. In the first place *Matan Torah* is to the nation, not to the individual. Therefore, *Thus shall you speak to* BEIS YAAKOV. It is first and foremost as a nation that we are called upon to listen to the *kol* and to abide by the covenant. It is as a nation that we will become God's *segulah* and as a nation that we will aspire to become a *Mamleches Kohanim VeGoy Kadosh*.[5] However, a nation is built from individuals. In the real world it is man the lonely who gulps Torah into his innards, makes her his bride, and triumphantly brings her into his home. The BENEI YISRAEL, the individual Jews, are very much a part of the *simchah*.[6]

And, let us make sure that even the following nuance is not lost to us. Let us remember that in the Chazal that Rashi quotes, the one that identifies *Beis Yaakov* with the women and *Benei Yisrael* with the men, the expression *tomar* (used for the women)[7] is described as a soft, caressing form of address while *tageid* (used for the men)[8] is said to be almost harsh and certainly uncompromising. That shading remains true even if our contention is correct that the *peshuto shel mikra* demands that the sentence must be translated along the lines that I have suggested. For surely it is true that while the Ribono shel Olam may be stern and sometimes unforgiving to the individual who stands before Him to be judged, He will usually show mercy to the community for whom the "merit of the many"[9] holds sway.[10]

The time has come to bring this book to a close. For one last time I want to make an accounting of all the hours I spent this past year to gain some clarity in this *sugia*. Can I claim to have attained a more solid understanding of *Ma'amad Har Sinai?* I think that I have and it is this: That the Ribono shel Olam gave us *Aseres HaDibros* from Har Sinai is clear and this I knew before I began writing this book. What I found out as a result of my serious learning of the *sugia* is that this is not the whole story. It is not the whole story in the same way that the fact that the Chasan handed the Kallah a ring could never be the whole story of a Chasunah. When we dance at a wedding we are celebrating the birth of a new complex personality—the melding of two discrete personalities into a new exquisite whole. Let us remember the reason that the Ribono shel Olam gave for bringing us to Sinai: ואביא אתכם אלי, *I brought you unto Me.* He did not mention that it was at Sinai that He intended to give us *Aseres HaDibros*. I have made this phrase the title of this book because, as I see it, these words tell the whole story.

It all started with the Ramban whose acquaintance we made first in chapter 2 and who has accompanied us in most of the chapters that followed. By breaking away from most of the other *Meforshim* and interpreting *and guard my covenant* of Shemos 19:5 as referring to the *bris* that the Ribono shel Olam had made with Avraham that He would be our God and we would be His people, Ramban placed the establishment of the relationship of ourselves to the Ribono shel Olam, squarely at the center of *Ma'amad Har Sinai*. More than any of the other standard *Meforshim,* Ramban affirmed the Chasunah nature of *Ma'amad Har Sinai.*[11] Everything else followed from that all-powerful premise.

We have one more port of call to make. There is another piece of Chumash that we need to study through the eyes of the Ramban. It will confirm much of what we have learned in this book. We will build our case step by step. In the end it will have been well worth the trip.

We will be thinking about Devarim 26:16–19, a passage which is clearly meant to be a kind of finale to Moshe Rabbeinu's function as the Rebbe of Klal Yisrael. The time has come to say good-bye. What is he going to say? When he has gone, the sun will have set.[12] Its warm, life-generating light will have sunk, irretrievably, beyond the horizon. All that will be left is a cold, uncaring moon, helpful to an extent because it still reflects the sun's brightness, but it is a light that loses much in translation. A world without Moshe Rabbeinu is not a lesser but an altogether different world. There is no doubt that Moshe Rabbeinu is indispensable, but—and here's the rub—he must make himself dispensable. He has given himself only four short verses within which to work his magic. What does he do? What does he say?

Perhaps the following idea has some merit. While Moshe Rabbeinu is with them, he stands *between* them and the Ribono shel Olam.[13] As he readies himself and them for the final farewell, he has a last gift to give them. It is the gift of spiritual self-reliance. It is the knowledge that, with the complete Torah in hand, they can stand on their own before their God. I suppose that we could word this insight as does Mechilta, Yisro 1: *Moshe Rabbeinu's worth is equivalent to that of the "six hundred thousand." The worth of the "six hundred thousand" is equivalent to that of Moshe Rabbeinu.*

Here is the passage upon which we will now focus.

היום הזה יהוה אלהיך מצוך לעשות את החקים האלה ואת המשפטים ושמרת ועשית אותם בכל לבבך ובכל נפשך. את יהוה האמרת היום להיות לך לאלהים וללכת בדרכיו ולשמר חקיו ומצותיו ומשפטיו ולשמע בקלו. ויהוה האמירך היום להיות לו לעם סגלה כאשר דבר לך ולשמר כל מצותיו. ולתתך עליון על כל הגוים אשר עשה לתהלה ולשם ולתפארת ולהיתך עם קדש ליהוה אלהיך כאשר דבר.

On this day, HaShem your God commands you to act in accordance with all the statutes and the laws. Be conscientious and perform them with all your heart and all your soul. Today you have exalted[14] HaShem to be your God, to walk in His ways and to be conscientious in keeping His statutes and His commands and His laws and to obey all that He commands you. And HaShem has exalted you today to be a very special people (*segulah*) to Him, in accordance with that which He said, and to obey His commandments. And to make you supreme among the nations that He has made that you should be an object of praise and of fame and of majesty and that you should be a nation cleaving to Him Who is Holy,[15] as He has spoken (Devarim 26:16).

The implications of this passage are so profound that we have to study it very carefully. A chart will help.

<table>
<tr><td colspan="2">טז. היום הזה ה' אלהיך מצוך לעשות את החקים האלה ואת המשפטים ושמרת ועשית אותם בכל לבבך ובכל נפשך</td><td>A</td></tr>
<tr><td>יח. וה' האמירך היום להיות לו לעם סגלה כאשר דבר לך</td><td>יז. את ה' האמרת היום להיות לך לאלהים</td><td>B</td></tr>
<tr><td>ולשמר כל מצותיו</td><td>וללכת בדרכיו</td><td>C</td></tr>
<tr><td>יט. ולתתך עליון על כל הגוים אשר עשה לתהלה ולשם ולתפארת ולהיתך עם קדש לה' אלהיך כאשר דבר</td><td>ולשמר חקיו ומצותיו ומשפטיו ולשמע בקלו</td><td>D</td></tr>
</table>

We note that the A section is not divided into two columns, while the B, C, and D sections are. This is so because the A section, which comprises the whole of verse 16, is an introduction to what follows. Verses 17–19 then describe how the Ribono shel Olam and Klal Yisrael each exalted the other in the ways that are spelled out in the C and D sections. These two exaltations, God's exaltation of Israel and Israel's exaltation of the Ribono shel Olam, have much in common and it is in order to make those commonalities clear that we divided the two into columns and placed them next to each other. Structured thus, it will be easier to appreciate the similarities.

By now it will have become clear that the mutual exalting that is described in verses 17–19 is the result of what was said in verse 16. Our immediate task will be to examine what precisely verse 16 is saying. Here is what Ramban says:

> ON THIS DAY, HASHEM YOUR GOD COMMANDS YOU TO ACT . . . Please note that at this point Moshe Rabbeinu has completed the explanation of the whole Torah, including all the *mitzvos* contained in Sefer Devarim that had not been taught previously. It is because everything was now known that he said, "On this day, HaShem your God commands you to act in accordance with the statutes and the laws . . ." because now there was nothing more to add.

This was a unique moment in Jewish history. It is true that the Israelites had been given new *mitzvos* throughout their forty years of wilderness travel. But never, before this moment, had they known *all* the *mitzvos*. As Ramban will say in his remarks to verse 18 that we will quote a little further down, "For this day is like another Sinai experience for you." Why is that so? How does Sinai enter into things at this stage? Where is the Fire-Gushing Mountain? Where are the claps of thunder, the lightning and the darkening clouds? Where is the voice of the Ribono shel Olam communicating with us from within the flames? If all the props are missing, how is this the same play?

Well, it is not really the same play, any more than the mature warmth, and yes, the love, between a couple married for many decades is the same as the ardor of youth when Chasan and Kallah first enter the Chupah. There is no comparison, is there? But, then again, it is the same, is it not? Deeper, yes. More profound and more solid, yes. But in essence, of course, it is the same. The trappings are missing because no one misses them. The band, the photographer, the flowers have become unnecessary. They were needed to drown out the question marks that like ghouls at a party would spoil the fun. In the maturity won through the years of togetherness, those question marks have long disappeared. The facts themselves are all that is needed.

At Sinai we all stood, Jewishly young, with very little idea of what becoming a *Mamleches Kohanim VeGoy Kadosh* would entail. In the rapture of the anticipation of meeting, so to speak, face-to-face with the Ribono shel Olam, the Chasan, we, to our eternal credit, found it in ourselves to say *Na'aseh VeNishma*. It was a *Kabbalas HaTorah* built on *bitachon*. The *Kabbalas HaTorah* was now repeated in Arvos Moav, but this time the reliance upon *bitachon* had become unnecessary. The comfortable knowledge of total compatibility was able to carry the day.

It carried the day and precipitated the mutual exalting that is now about to be described. By accepting the Torah in its entirety, we apparently entered into a relationship with the Ribono shel Olam that had not existed earlier. By glancing at the B, C, and D sections on the right side of the above chart, it becomes clear that our exalting of the Ribono shel Olam at this stage of the relationship resulted in four distinct obligations of which, please note, the keeping of His commands comes in only as the third.

Here is a small chart that will illustrate how Ramban views each of these four obligations:

You have exalted Him in the sense that He alone will be your God, that under no circumstances (כלל) would you ever give credence (לא תודו) to any other power (באל אחר).	להיות לך לאלהים To be your God
That your actions will be good and fair, and that you practice kindness among yourselves.	וללכת בדרכיו To walk in His ways
	ולשמור חוקיו ומצותיו ומשפטיו And to obey His statutes, His commands and His civil laws.
Whatever else He might command you either through me [Moshe Rabbeinu] or through His other prophets.	ולשמוע בקלו And to listen to His voice

After the Torah tells us how we exalted the Ribono shel Olam, it moves on to teach us in what sense the Ribono shel Olam exalted us. Once more, we will provide a chart in order to the better facilitate a comparison between the two.[16]

"Today" because this day [upon which they had finally received the entire Torah] was like another "Sinai" experience for them. So [on this day] God exalted them through their acceptance of the Torah, that they would now become His special love (סגולה) among all the nations.	וה' האמירך היום להיות לו לעם סגולה . . . And HaShem exalted you today to become His special love . . .
For it is only to you that He gives His Torah, it is only you whom He commands to live by those standards that He deems to be correct. He does none of this to any other nation.	ולשמור כל מצוותיו And to obey His commandments.
"An object of praise" is meant in the sense that all the nations of the world will admire your closeness to the Ribono shel Olam as is testified by the fact that whenever you call out to Him in prayer, He answers you.[17]	ולתתך עליון . . . לתהלה . . . To place you above all the nations in order that you should be an object of praise . . .
And your renown will go forth among the nations for His splendor that He has placed upon you, for you are exalted above all.[18]	ולשם . . . And to grant you fame . . .
For you will be glorified over them by being able to do with them whatever you desire . . .	ולתפארת And glory . . .
The implication of "עם קדוש" is that even after death you will be granted eternal life, cleaving to the Ribono shel Olam.	ולהיותך עם קדוש . . . כאשר דבר And to be a holy nation . . . in accordance with that which he has spoken.

Some Answers to Some Significant Questions

We have now reached the point at which we can usefully compare the two "exaltations," Israel's exaltation of the Ribono shel Olam and the Ribono shel Olam's exaltation of Israel, and draw some important conclusions.

Here we come with the final chart.

ISRAEL'S EXALTATION OF THE RIBONO SHEL OLAM	THE RIBONO SHEL OLAM'S EXALTATION OF ISRAEL
1. You have exalted Him in the sense that He alone will be your God, that under no circumstances (כלל) would you ever give credence (לא תודו) to any other power (באל אחר).	"Today" because this day [upon which they had finally received the entire Torah] was like another "Sinai" experience for them. So [on this day] God exalted them through their acceptance of the Torah, that they would now become His special love (סגולה) among all the nations.
2.	For it is only to you that He gives His Torah, it is only you whom He commands to live by those standards that He deems to be correct. He does none of this to any other nation.
3. That your actions be good and fair, and that you practice kindness among yourselves.	"An object of praise" is meant in the sense that all the nations of the world will admire your closeness to the Ribono shel Olam as is testified by the fact that whenever you call out to Him in prayer, He answers you.[19]
4. And to obey His statutes, His commands, and His civil laws. [This is the Torah's language, not that of the Ramban. Ramban's comments to this phrase are not germane to our argument.]	And your renown will go forth among the nations for His splendor that He has placed upon you, for you are exalted above all.
5. Whatever else He might command you either through me [Moshe Rabbeinu] or through His other prophets.	For you will be glorified over them by being able to do with them whatever you desire ... The implication of "עם קדוש" is that even after death you will be granted eternal life, cleaving to the Ribono shel Olam.

Numbers 3, 4, and 5 offer no real surprises. Klal Yisrael exalts the Ribono shel Olam by undertaking to fulfill all their obligations conscientiously. That is precisely what we would expect once they had received the Torah in its entirety. The Ribono shel Olam responds by promising that in return for their meticulous attention to their obligations, he would shower them with privileges that would testify to their very special standing among the nations of the world.

Numbers 1 (in the case of Israel's exaltation of the Ribono shel Olam) and 1 and 2 (in the case of the Ribono shel Olam's exaltation of Israel) are, by contrast, very significant in the context of themes that we have discussed throughout this book. Their common thrust is the exclusivity of their commitments to each other. Israel declares its fidelity to *only* the Ribono shel Olam and makes much of the fact that *under no circumstances* would it consider giving credence to any other power. The Ribono shel Olam in number 1 invokes the *segulah* concept with all its exclusionary connotations, and in number 2 makes these implications explicit by stressing the fact that He gave His precious Torah to only Klal Yisrael and to no one else.

If we now recall Ramban's remark that the day upon which the final *mitzvos* were given was, in effect, a second "*Ma'amad Har Sinai,*" then we have a significant confirmation of the thesis that we have been propounding throughout this book. Based on the Ramban concerning the Yisro *bris,*[20] we argued that the Sinaitic experience was first and foremost a coming together of the Ribono shel Olam with Klal Yisrael, or as Chazal put it, a Chasunah. It transpires that *Aseres HaDibros,* in and of themselves, do not fill the entire Sinaitic stage. They are part of a much larger picture. The day of *Matan Torah* was the day of the wedding between the Ribono shel Olam and Klal Yisrael. *Aseres HaDibros,* by laying down the constitutional principles that were to govern God's *segulah,* would serve as the guarantee that we would indeed walk through history as a *Mamleches Kohanim VeGoy Kadosh.*

And once we know that, we can return to another of the questions that we left open in chapter 1. We recall that verse 4 of the Ribono shel Olam's introductory communication at Har Sinai reminded us of what He had done to the Egyptians for our sake and stressed how He had brought us to Him upon the wings of eagles. Here, once more, is the question that we asked there.

> From the point of view of its content, verse 4 is unproblematic. The message of love and caring that it conveys could not be clearer. If there is a problem it is one of "Why?" not one of "What?" Why mention this here? Why would this have any bearing upon *Ma'amad Har Sinai?*[21] The answer is not obvious and we must live with the fact that we will not understand verse 4 correctly until we win a better understanding of what was about to happen.

It all seems so simple now. Let us ask ourselves what is really the *p'shuto shel mikra,* the simple meaning of this verse? The Rashi that I have presented for your consideration in note 21 is so beloved by all of us, is, because of its warmth and caring, so well known to us, that we tend to ignore the fact that it cannot really be viewed as being actually yielded by the plain text. As Midrash, it does precisely what Midrash is supposed to do. It provides the background with which the *p'shat* cannot deal. But, and this we must ask in all earnestness, what *is* the *p'shat*? Why is it that on a passage concerning which Rashi waxes so eloquent, Ramban is completely silent? It is because the verse means exactly what it appears to mean; nothing need be said because the text says it all. The verse is saying that bringing you to Me was very important to Me, so important that I was willing to smash Mitzrayim with My plagues and bring you here on eagles' wings. I "needed" you, I wanted you, and so I brought you. I allowed nothing to stand in my way.

It is not for nothing that I chose the phrase, *And I brought you unto Me* (Shemos 19:4) as the title of this book. When we consider that it is with these words that the Ribono shel Olam welcomed us to Sinai,[22] emphasizing that all that he did to the Egyptians and the love that He displayed by bearing us on the "wings of eagles," was all for just this one purpose, that He might be together with us,[23] it becomes very clear what *Ma'amad Har Sinai* is all about.[24] Let us think about the implications. Let us think of what the Ribono shel Olam is teaching us with those three simple words:

ואביא אתכם אלי

I have just one more idea to share with you and then we will be done.

We have been dealing with Ramban's idea that the day upon which *Matan Torah* was completed had the character of a second *Ma'amad Har Sinai*. Ramban does not make the following point, but it seems clear to me that the language that the Torah chooses in the passage that we have been discussing fully bears out his contention. In verse 18 we have, *And HaShem exalted you this day to be an* AM SEGULAH for Him, and verse 19 concludes with the words, *And that you shall become a* NATION CLEAVING TO HIM WHO IS HOLY *for HaShem your God as He had spoken*. If you have struggled along throughout this book with me, you will by now be very familiar with the triad, *segulah, Mamleches Kohanim,* and *Goy Kadosh* that stand at the center of the Sinaitic experience. And, being familiar with them, you will surely share my perplexity at the missing *Mamleches Kohanim*. Why do only two of the three, but not the third, appear in our context.

I have not seen anyone else ask this question, but it troubles me. I suppose that, having lived with these ideas for quite a while during the gestation period of this book, I have become particularly sensitive to the implications.

I have the following suggestion to make. If you glance back at the relevant verses and take another look at the various charts that deal with the Ribono shel Olam's exaltation of Klal Yisrael, you will note the very first praise that He utters is the promise that we are to become his *Am Segulah*. The last words that He says are the ones that tell us that we are to become an *Am Kadosh*.

It is my contention that just as in Yisro, *Mamleches Kohanim* comes between these two accolades, so too, in the Arvos Moav passage, the part in between *segulah* and *Am Kadosh* is there in place of the *Mamleches Kohanim.* The difference is only that, whereas in Yisro the term is spelled out, here it is described. To be granted that we become an *object of praise,* that our *fame* and *glory* would become known to the nations of the world, that *is* the meaning of becoming a *Mamleches Kohanim.* We recall that Rashi translated *Kohanim* in this context as *princes.* God's promise is that Klal Yisrael is to be an aristocracy. It is the Jewish aristocrat who is being described in the passage under discussion.

And it is as *sarim,* as aristocrats, that we will come out to welcome Melech HaMoshi'ach. Let us work hard to become the kind of people about whom it will be true to say that they live by standards that galvanize the entire world to look upon them as role models.[25]

לתהלה ולשם ולתפארת

ולהיתך עם קדוש לה' אלהיך

SHEMOS, CHAPTER 19

א. בַּחֹדֶשׁ הַשְּׁלִישִׁי לְצֵאת בְּנֵי יִשְׂרָאֵל מֵאֶרֶץ מִצְרָיִם בַּיּוֹם הַזֶּה בָּאוּ מִדְבַּר סִינָי: ב. וַיִּסְעוּ מֵרְפִידִים וַיָּבֹאוּ מִדְבַּר סִינַי וַיַּחֲנוּ בַּמִּדְבָּר וַיִּחַן שָׁם יִשְׂרָאֵל נֶגֶד הָהָר: ג. וּמֹשֶׁה עָלָה אֶל הָאֱלֹהִים וַיִּקְרָא אֵלָיו יְהוָה מִן הָהָר לֵאמֹר כֹּה תֹאמַר לְבֵית יַעֲקֹב וְתַגֵּיד לִבְנֵי יִשְׂרָאֵל: ד. אַתֶּם רְאִיתֶם אֲשֶׁר עָשִׂיתִי לְמִצְרָיִם וָאֶשָּׂא אֶתְכֶם עַל כַּנְפֵי נְשָׁרִים וָאָבִא אֶתְכֶם אֵלָי: ה. וְעַתָּה אִם שָׁמוֹעַ תִּשְׁמְעוּ בְּקֹלִי וּשְׁמַרְתֶּם אֶת בְּרִיתִי וִהְיִיתֶם לִי סְגֻלָּה מִכָּל הָעַמִּים כִּי לִי כָּל הָאָרֶץ: ו. וְאַתֶּם תִּהְיוּ לִי מַמְלֶכֶת כֹּהֲנִים וְגוֹי קָדוֹשׁ אֵלֶּה הַדְּבָרִים אֲשֶׁר תְּדַבֵּר אֶל בְּנֵי יִשְׂרָאֵל: ז. וַיָּבֹא מֹשֶׁה וַיִּקְרָא לְזִקְנֵי הָעָם וַיָּשֶׂם לִפְנֵיהֶם אֵת כָּל הַדְּבָרִים הָאֵלֶּה אֲשֶׁר צִוָּהוּ יְהוָה: ח. וַיַּעֲנוּ כָל הָעָם יַחְדָּו וַיֹּאמְרוּ כֹּל אֲשֶׁר דִּבֶּר יְהוָה נַעֲשֶׂה וַיָּשֶׁב מֹשֶׁה אֶת דִּבְרֵי הָעָם אֶל יְהוָה: ט. וַיֹּאמֶר יְהוָה אֶל מֹשֶׁה הִנֵּה אָנֹכִי בָּא אֵלֶיךָ בְּעַב הֶעָנָן בַּעֲבוּר יִשְׁמַע הָעָם בְּדַבְּרִי עִמָּךְ וְגַם בְּךָ יַאֲמִינוּ לְעוֹלָם וַיַּגֵּד מֹשֶׁה אֶת דִּבְרֵי הָעָם אֶל יְהוָה: י. וַיֹּאמֶר יְהוָה אֶל מֹשֶׁה לֵךְ אֶל הָעָם וְקִדַּשְׁתָּם הַיּוֹם וּמָחָר וְכִבְּסוּ שִׂמְלֹתָם: יא. וְהָיוּ נְכֹנִים לַיּוֹם הַשְּׁלִישִׁי כִּי בַּיּוֹם הַשְּׁלִשִׁי יֵרֵד יְהוָה לְעֵינֵי כָל הָעָם עַל הַר סִינָי: יב. וְהִגְבַּלְתָּ אֶת הָעָם סָבִיב לֵאמֹר הִשָּׁמְרוּ לָכֶם עֲלוֹת בָּהָר וּנְגֹעַ בְּקָצֵהוּ כָּל הַנֹּגֵעַ בָּהָר מוֹת יוּמָת: יג. לֹא תִגַּע בּוֹ יָד כִּי סָקוֹל יִסָּקֵל אוֹ יָרֹה יִיָּרֶה אִם בְּהֵמָה אִם אִישׁ לֹא יִחְיֶה בִּמְשֹׁךְ הַיֹּבֵל הֵמָּה יַעֲלוּ בָהָר: יד. וַיֵּרֶד מֹשֶׁה מִן הָהָר אֶל הָעָם וַיְקַדֵּשׁ אֶת הָעָם וַיְכַבְּסוּ שִׂמְלֹתָם: טו. וַיֹּאמֶר אֶל הָעָם הֱיוּ נְכֹנִים לִשְׁלֹשֶׁת יָמִים אַל תִּגְּשׁוּ אֶל אִשָּׁה: טז. וַיְהִי בַיּוֹם הַשְּׁלִישִׁי בִּהְיֹת הַבֹּקֶר וַיְהִי קֹלֹת וּבְרָקִים וְעָנָן כָּבֵד עַל הָהָר וְקֹל שֹׁפָר חָזָק מְאֹד וַיֶּחֱרַד כָּל הָעָם אֲשֶׁר בַּמַּחֲנֶה: יז. וַיּוֹצֵא מֹשֶׁה אֶת הָעָם לִקְרַאת הָאֱלֹהִים מִן הַמַּחֲנֶה וַיִּתְיַצְּבוּ בְּתַחְתִּית הָהָר: יח. וְהַר סִינַי עָשַׁן כֻּלּוֹ מִפְּנֵי אֲשֶׁר יָרַד עָלָיו יְהוָה בָּאֵשׁ וַיַּעַל עֲשָׁנוֹ כְּעֶשֶׁן הַכִּבְשָׁן וַיֶּחֱרַד כָּל הָהָר מְאֹד: יט. וַיְהִי קוֹל הַשֹּׁפָר הוֹלֵךְ וְחָזֵק מְאֹד מֹשֶׁה יְדַבֵּר וְהָאֱלֹהִים יַעֲנֶנּוּ בְקוֹל: כ. וַיֵּרֶד יְהוָה עַל הַר סִינַי אֶל רֹאשׁ הָהָר וַיִּקְרָא יְהוָה לְמֹשֶׁה אֶל רֹאשׁ הָהָר וַיַּעַל מֹשֶׁה: כא. וַיֹּאמֶר יְהוָה אֶל מֹשֶׁה רֵד הָעֵד בָּעָם פֶּן יֶהֶרְסוּ אֶל יְהוָה לִרְאוֹת וְנָפַל מִמֶּנּוּ רָב: כב. וְגַם הַכֹּהֲנִים הַנִּגָּשִׁים אֶל יְהוָה יִתְקַדָּשׁוּ פֶּן יִפְרֹץ בָּהֶם יְהוָה: כג. וַיֹּאמֶר מֹשֶׁה אֶל יְהוָה לֹא יוּכַל הָעָם לַעֲלֹת אֶל הַר סִינָי כִּי אַתָּה הַעֵדֹתָה בָּנוּ לֵאמֹר הַגְבֵּל אֶת הָהָר וְקִדַּשְׁתּוֹ: כד. וַיֹּאמֶר אֵלָיו יְהוָה לֶךְ רֵד וְעָלִיתָ אַתָּה וְאַהֲרֹן עִמָּךְ וְהַכֹּהֲנִים וְהָעָם אַל יֶהֶרְסוּ לַעֲלֹת אֶל יְהוָה פֶּן יִפְרָץ בָּם: כה. וַיֵּרֶד מֹשֶׁה אֶל הָעָם וַיֹּאמֶר אֲלֵהֶם:

SHEMOS, CHAPTER 20

א. וַיְדַבֵּר אֱלֹהִים אֵת כָּל הַדְּבָרִים הָאֵלֶּה לֵאמֹר: ב. אָנֹכִי יְהוָה אֱלֹהֶיךָ אֲשֶׁר הוֹצֵאתִיךָ מֵאֶרֶץ מִצְרַיִם מִבֵּית עֲבָדִים לֹא יִהְיֶה לְךָ אֱלֹהִים אֲחֵרִים עַל פָּנָי: ג. לֹא תַעֲשֶׂה לְךָ פֶסֶל וְכָל תְּמוּנָה אֲשֶׁר בַּשָּׁמַיִם מִמַּעַל וַאֲשֶׁר בָּאָרֶץ מִתַּחַת וַאֲשֶׁר בַּמַּיִם מִתַּחַת לָאָרֶץ: ד. לֹא תִשְׁתַּחֲוֶה לָהֶם וְלֹא תָעָבְדֵם כִּי אָנֹכִי יְהוָה אֱלֹהֶיךָ אֵל קַנָּא פֹּקֵד עֲוֹן אָבֹת עַל בָּנִים עַל שִׁלֵּשִׁים וְעַל רִבֵּעִים לְשֹׂנְאָי: ה. וְעֹשֶׂה חֶסֶד לַאֲלָפִים לְאֹהֲבַי וּלְשֹׁמְרֵי מִצְוֹתָי: ו. לֹא תִשָּׂא אֶת שֵׁם יְהוָה אֱלֹהֶיךָ לַשָּׁוְא כִּי לֹא יְנַקֶּה יְהוָה אֵת אֲשֶׁר יִשָּׂא אֶת שְׁמוֹ לַשָּׁוְא: ז. זָכוֹר אֶת יוֹם הַשַּׁבָּת לְקַדְּשׁוֹ: ח. שֵׁשֶׁת יָמִים תַּעֲבֹד

וְעָשִׂיתָ כָּל מְלַאכְתֶּךָ: ט. וְיוֹם הַשְּׁבִיעִי שַׁבָּת לַיהֹוָה אֱלֹהֶיךָ לֹא תַעֲשֶׂה כָל מְלָאכָה
אַתָּה וּבִנְךָ וּבִתֶּךָ עַבְדְּךָ וַאֲמָתְךָ וּבְהֶמְתֶּךָ וְגֵרְךָ אֲשֶׁר בִּשְׁעָרֶיךָ: י. כִּי שֵׁשֶׁת יָמִים עָשָׂה
יְהֹוָה אֶת הַשָּׁמַיִם וְאֶת הָאָרֶץ אֶת הַיָּם וְאֶת כָּל אֲשֶׁר בָּם וַיָּנַח בַּיּוֹם הַשְּׁבִיעִי עַל כֵּן
בֵּרַךְ יְהֹוָה אֶת יוֹם הַשַּׁבָּת וַיְקַדְּשֵׁהוּ: יא. כַּבֵּד אֶת אָבִיךָ וְאֶת אִמֶּךָ לְמַעַן יַאֲרִכוּן
יָמֶיךָ עַל הָאֲדָמָה אֲשֶׁר יְהֹוָה אֱלֹהֶיךָ נֹתֵן לָךְ: יב. לֹא תִרְצָח לֹא תִנְאָף לֹא תִגְנֹב לֹא
תַעֲנֶה בְרֵעֲךָ עֵד שָׁקֶר: יג. לֹא תַחְמֹד בֵּית רֵעֶךָ לֹא תַחְמֹד אֵשֶׁת רֵעֶךָ וְעַבְדּוֹ וַאֲמָתוֹ
וְשׁוֹרוֹ וַחֲמֹרוֹ וְכֹל אֲשֶׁר לְרֵעֶךָ: יד. וְכָל הָעָם רֹאִים אֶת הַקּוֹלֹת וְאֶת הַלַּפִּידִם וְאֵת
קוֹל הַשֹּׁפָר וְאֶת הָהָר עָשֵׁן וַיַּרְא הָעָם וַיָּנֻעוּ וַיַּעַמְדוּ מֵרָחֹק: טו. וַיֹּאמְרוּ אֶל מֹשֶׁה
דַּבֵּר אַתָּה עִמָּנוּ וְנִשְׁמָעָה וְאַל יְדַבֵּר עִמָּנוּ אֱלֹהִים פֶּן נָמוּת: טז. וַיֹּאמֶר מֹשֶׁה אֶל
הָעָם אַל תִּירָאוּ כִּי לְבַעֲבוּר נַסּוֹת אֶתְכֶם בָּא הָאֱלֹהִים וּבַעֲבוּר תִּהְיֶה יִרְאָתוֹ עַל
פְּנֵיכֶם לְבִלְתִּי תֶחֱטָאוּ: יז. וַיַּעֲמֹד הָעָם מֵרָחֹק וּמֹשֶׁה נִגַּשׁ אֶל הָעֲרָפֶל אֲשֶׁר שָׁם
הָאֱלֹהִים: יח. וַיֹּאמֶר יְהֹוָה אֶל מֹשֶׁה כֹּה תֹאמַר אֶל בְּנֵי יִשְׂרָאֵל אַתֶּם רְאִיתֶם כִּי
מִן הַשָּׁמַיִם דִּבַּרְתִּי עִמָּכֶם: יט. לֹא תַעֲשׂוּן אִתִּי אֱלֹהֵי כֶסֶף וֵאלֹהֵי זָהָב לֹא תַעֲשׂוּ
לָכֶם: כ. מִזְבַּח אֲדָמָה תַּעֲשֶׂה לִּי וְזָבַחְתָּ עָלָיו אֶת עֹלֹתֶיךָ וְאֶת שְׁלָמֶיךָ אֶת צֹאנְךָ
וְאֶת בְּקָרֶךָ בְּכָל הַמָּקוֹם אֲשֶׁר אַזְכִּיר אֶת שְׁמִי אָבוֹא אֵלֶיךָ וּבֵרַכְתִּיךָ: כא. וְאִם מִזְבַּח
אֲבָנִים תַּעֲשֶׂה לִּי לֹא תִבְנֶה אֶתְהֶן גָּזִית כִּי חַרְבְּךָ הֵנַפְתָּ עָלֶיהָ וַתְּחַלְלֶהָ: כב. וְלֹא
תַעֲלֶה בְמַעֲלֹת עַל מִזְבְּחִי אֲשֶׁר לֹא תִגָּלֶה עֶרְוָתְךָ עָלָיו:

SHEMOS, CHAPTER 21

א. וְאֵלֶּה הַמִּשְׁפָּטִים אֲשֶׁר תָּשִׂים לִפְנֵיהֶם:

SHEMOS, CHAPTER 24

א. וְאֶל מֹשֶׁה אָמַר עֲלֵה אֶל יְהֹוָה אַתָּה וְאַהֲרֹן נָדָב וַאֲבִיהוּא וְשִׁבְעִים מִזִּקְנֵי יִשְׂרָאֵל
וְהִשְׁתַּחֲוִיתֶם מֵרָחֹק: ב. וְנִגַּשׁ מֹשֶׁה לְבַדּוֹ אֶל יְהֹוָה וְהֵם לֹא יִגָּשׁוּ וְהָעָם לֹא יַעֲלוּ
עִמּוֹ: ג. וַיָּבֹא מֹשֶׁה וַיְסַפֵּר לָעָם אֵת כָּל דִּבְרֵי יְהֹוָה וְאֵת כָּל הַמִּשְׁפָּטִים וַיַּעַן כָּל הָעָם
קוֹל אֶחָד וַיֹּאמְרוּ כָּל הַדְּבָרִים אֲשֶׁר דִּבֶּר יְהֹוָה נַעֲשֶׂה: ד. וַיִּכְתֹּב מֹשֶׁה אֵת כָּל דִּבְרֵי
יְהֹוָה וַיַּשְׁכֵּם בַּבֹּקֶר וַיִּבֶן מִזְבֵּחַ תַּחַת הָהָר וּשְׁתֵּים עֶשְׂרֵה מַצֵּבָה לִשְׁנֵים עָשָׂר שִׁבְטֵי
יִשְׂרָאֵל: ה. וַיִּשְׁלַח אֶת נַעֲרֵי בְּנֵי יִשְׂרָאֵל וַיַּעֲלוּ עֹלֹת וַיִּזְבְּחוּ זְבָחִים שְׁלָמִים לַיהֹוָה
פָּרִים: ו. וַיִּקַּח מֹשֶׁה חֲצִי הַדָּם וַיָּשֶׂם בָּאַגָּנֹת וַחֲצִי הַדָּם זָרַק עַל הַמִּזְבֵּחַ: ז. וַיִּקַּח
סֵפֶר הַבְּרִית וַיִּקְרָא בְּאָזְנֵי הָעָם וַיֹּאמְרוּ כֹּל אֲשֶׁר דִּבֶּר יְהֹוָה נַעֲשֶׂה וְנִשְׁמָע: ח. וַיִּקַּח
מֹשֶׁה אֶת הַדָּם וַיִּזְרֹק עַל הָעָם וַיֹּאמֶר הִנֵּה דַם הַבְּרִית אֲשֶׁר כָּרַת יְהֹוָה עִמָּכֶם עַל כָּל
הַדְּבָרִים הָאֵלֶּה: ט. וַיַּעַל מֹשֶׁה וְאַהֲרֹן נָדָב וַאֲבִיהוּא וְשִׁבְעִים מִזִּקְנֵי יִשְׂרָאֵל: י. וַיִּרְאוּ
אֵת אֱלֹהֵי יִשְׂרָאֵל וְתַחַת רַגְלָיו כְּמַעֲשֵׂה לִבְנַת הַסַּפִּיר וּכְעֶצֶם הַשָּׁמַיִם לָטֹהַר: יא. וְאֶל
אֲצִילֵי בְּנֵי יִשְׂרָאֵל לֹא שָׁלַח יָדוֹ וַיֶּחֱזוּ אֶת הָאֱלֹהִים וַיֹּאכְלוּ וַיִּשְׁתּוּ:

NOTES

PREFACE *A Look at Where We Are Headed*

1 I apologize for the use of this rather inelegant phrase. It is one that somehow stuck in my mind from years when I was teaching high school in the Philadelphia Yeshiva. It was spoken by a beloved *Talmid* who grew up to become a Talmid Chacham and a master Rebbi. R. Yehudah Naftali Mandelbaum was *niftar* as a young father of a wonderful family in the middle of a teaching career that showed enormous promise. There are many people who, even after the many years that have passed since then, miss him sadly.
This was in tenth grade and I had just done a really good job of explaining a particularly difficult passage—or at least so I was telling myself. Yehudah Naftali disabused me quickly enough. "Rebbi," he said, "I don't understand a word. I am one big blob of confusion." The phrase stuck with me and I use it now as a gesture of fond farewell to a great Ben Torah.

2 Well, not really on that day. Herewith I offer a short explanation. There is a difference of opinion between Tana'im (Shabbos 86b) about the day on which the Ribono shel Olam gave us the *Aseres HaDibros*. The Rabanan maintain that it was on the sixth of Sivan while R. Yose thinks that it was on the seventh. There are certain halachic issues that depend on the outcome of this debate, the details of which need not detain us here. The *halachah* is decided in favor of R. Yose and, accordingly we must assume that it was the seventh of Iyar upon which we heard *Aseres HaDibros*.
The way in which our calendar is arranged, Nisan has thirty days and Iyar has twenty-nine. You can do your own mathematics, which of course must be based upon the fact that we left Mitzrayim on the fifteenth of Nisan. You will find that the fiftieth day from the sixteenth of Nisan comes out on the sixth of Sivan. That is one day too early.
Before the *lu'ach* was fixed and Rosh Chodesh was determined through witnesses who testified that they had seen the new moon, there are more possibilities. Nisan and Iyar could have been: (a) both thirty days in which case Shavuos would have come out on the fifth of Sivan—that is, two days early; (b) one thirty and the other twenty-nine in which case Shavuos would have come out on the sixth of Iyar—one day early; or, (c) both twenty-nine, in which case Shavuos would have come out on the seventh of Iyar—on the exact day of *Matan Torah*.
It turns out that there is only a 1:2 chance that Shavuos would come out on the historical date upon which *Matan Torah* actually happened.
Now, much has been written about this issue and various explanations for this strange phenomenon have been offered. At the end of the day, the facts still appear strange. If the thoughts that I will be presenting are correct, that would make the problem much less troubling.

3 I am aware of the tradition that the ten *Dibros* can be viewed as *Avos*, "chiefs" of ten categories under which all the 613 *mitzvos* can be subsumed. It is difficult for me to credit this as sufficient justification for using the all-inclusive

term "Torah" for just these few *mitzvos*. As to why we refer to this Yom Tov as זמן מתן תורתנו, please see chapter 20 for a discussion of the term.

4 I say this in full awareness that in our תפילה we refer to Shavuos as "זמן "מתן תורתנו . That wording is actually quite problematic. The Mishnah in Ta'anis (4:8) uses "מתן תורה" to describe Yom Kippur, the day upon which we received (were given) the second *luchos* (Rashi to Shir HaShirim 3:11). In the Mishnah this is the only reference to מתן תורה. Now it is true that there are certain references to מתן תורה in the Gemara that clearly seem to have *Ma'amad Har Sinai* in mind. However, in view of the Tana'ic use of that term that we have just cited, that usage seems to me to be problematic. I have no real knowledge of the history of the usage of the term.

5 I have invented this term because it fits naturally into the family of twosomes and threesomes, which are perfectly good English words. In some of the dictionaries available to me the ". . . some" form goes up to seven but not beyond. I do not know why the language developed as it did.

6 בין אדם לחברו.

7 Shabbos 31a.

8 VaYikra 19:18.

9 Please see note 3 to chapter 7.

10 Please take a look at note 2 in this chapter. At this point of our discussion it will have become clear that the exact date on which we heard *Aseres HaDibros* is less important than we had thought. Since that event is only part of the larger drama of the Chasunah, an approximation is not at all out of place.

11 עיקר הדת וראשיתו in the standard translations. Kapach has יסוד הצווי ותחלתו.

12 In the present context I am not concerned with the question of how we convert a day that the Torah treats exclusively as a celebration of the harvest, into a זמן מתן תורתנו. A great deal has been written on this subject. There may be some among you readers who recall that I myself treated the issue in *A Pearl in the Sand,* my little book on Shavuos and Megilas Rus. Interested readers may find it useful to look at the Maharal, Tif'eres Yisrael 27.

13 In the Torah's number system, "seven" (because of its association with Shabbos) always describes the type of sanctity that testifies to the Ribono shel Olam's presence in this, our physical world. Seven times seven multiplies seven, seven times, thus jacking up the sanctity to its highest product.

14 We have not presented Rashi's explanation of the passage because that would have taken us much too far from where we needed to be heading, but I can at least mention that for him, this issue was very important and he dealt with it directly. In his scheme the invulnerability of the bush acted as a metaphor to assuage Moshe's fears of what would happen to him when he confronted Pharaoh. Bushlike, he too would be untouched by the dangers that inhere in bearding Pharaoh, the unscrupulous monster, in his lair. The bush was saved because it was God's faithful messenger. Moshe Rabbeinu would experience the same measure of protection. Even as the bush remained untouched, so would he.

NOTES

INTRODUCTION

1 שש זכירות.

2 זכירה from זכר, *to remember.*

3 למען תזכור את יום צאתך מארץ מצרים כל ימי חייך.

4 רק השמר לך ושמור נפשך מאד פן תשכח את הדברים אשר ראו עיניך ופן יסורו מלבבך כול ימי חייך והודעתם לבניך ולבני בניך יום אשר עמדת לפני ה' אלהיך בחרב.

5 See Ramban, Shemos 13:16, who explains why so many reminders are needed.

6 The Ramban to whom we pointed in note 5 explains the significance of the events that surrounded *Yetzi'as Mitzrayim* by explaining that each of the wonders that happened in those heady days was designed to teach us fundamental truths concerning the nature of the Ribono shel Olam: His omnipotence, His omniscience and so on. These are indeed truths of which we need to be reminded constantly. However, as we shall see throughout this book, *Ma'amad Har Sinai* has no less serious and significant implications. The very fact that it has a place of honor among the *shesh zechiros* indicates that its lessons must be our constant companion through life. So why not provide us with *mitzvos* that could give us a helping hand?

Now here is a secret that, since this morning, I am able to share with you. This morning I finally wrote the last paragraph of the book. This afternoon I began what for me is one of the most enjoyable aspects of authorship, the rewriting and polishing of what already exists. So now I know and now I can share it with you. The answer to the question that we have just now raised appears in chapter 21, the very last chapter. You could peek if you want, but I do not recommend it. The conclusions that I reach in that chapter are the fruits of very hard labor. It is worth your while to struggle along with me and then, when everything comes together, to savor the sweet taste of accomplishment.

ONE *Some Challenging Questions*

1 עתיקתא קשה מחדתא (Rashi, Yoma 29a).

2 For purely technical interest we note that God's charge to Moshe Rabbeinu, the passage with which we are dealing in this chapter, was made on the second of Sivan. Rosh Chodesh, the day upon which they arrived, was devoted to settling down. It was only on the next day that Moshe was called (Rashi).

3 At this point it is necessary to quote from the Maharal, Derech Chaim 3:2:

התורה כל דבריה מוכרחים ומחוייבים. אי אפשר רק שיהיה כך, ולא אפשר בענין אחר כלל, וזה מעלת התורה . . . כי אי אפשר שיהיה דבר אחר, אף נקודה אחת בתורה שאפשר שיהיה בענין אחר, רק כך. ואין לומר בתורה שראוי שיהיה כך אבל אינו מחוייב שיהיה כך, ואפשר שיהיה בענין אחר . . . דבר זו אינו בתורה.

Every single word in the Torah must be as it is and it is necessary that it be so. There is no possibility other than that it be precisely as it is, and that any other way would not and could not do. For it is impossible that there be one word in the Torah or even one dot in the Torah, that could conceivably have been different. It is impossible to think that a particular point which the Torah makes is well taken, a good idea, but it is not necessarily so. In the Torah this would be absolutely disallowed.

4 The Mechilta that is the source for Rashi's interpretation speaks of limiting the instruction of the women to ראשי פרקים, *general categories.*

5 This is how Ramban, Shemos 19:6, translates גוי קדוש.

6 This concept seems borne out by Tehilim 114:1, which is familiar to us from Hallel: בצאת ישראל ממצרים, בית יעקב מעם לעז. In this context it cannot possibly be claimed that "Yisrael" refers to the men and "Beis Yaakov" to the women.

7 וגוי אחד הם, וישכון בדד בשם יעקב וישראל . . . Rav Chavel adduces Devarim 33:28, וישכון **ישראל** בטח בדד עין **יעקב** . . . The background to Ramban's addition of these words is as follows. In the particular prophecy with which our passage deals, Bil'am says that Balak had invited him with the words, "Come curse *Yaakov* for me and call down wrath upon *Yisrael.*" Now that is simply not true on the literal level since, as told in the Chumash, the messengers had told Bil'am simply that Balak had said, "Behold 'a nation' has come out of Egypt," without identifying them as either "Yaakov" or "Yisrael." Ramban hints at the answer. The anonymous nation is clearly the Jewish nation. Since that nation, by definition, incorporates both the component "Yaakov" and the component "Yisrael," it was legitimate for Bil'am to use the poetic form that he did. It is as though Balak had actually said that Bil'am was being asked to curse both "Yaakov" and "Yisrael."

8 Ibn Ezra points out that we cannot assume that the femininity of "Beis Yaakov" lies in the use of "Beis" rather than in "Yaakov" as opposed to "Yisrael." Witness Tehilim 115:12, which speaks of "Beis Yisrael," and Tehilim 118:3, which speaks of "Beis Aaron." Both expressions occur also in Tehilim 135:19 (Ibn Ezra, Peirush HaKatzar, Shemos 19:3).

9 There is, of course, the unforgettable Rashi to this *pasuk*. Here is a paraphrase:

WHAT I DID TO MITZRAYIM: Long before you were involved with the Egyptians they had committed enough sins to have me punish them. I never did anything about it because they were of no importance to Me. Only once they were cruel to you did I release all My wrath against them. The message is one of love and caring. The earlier wickedness of the Egyptians meant nothing to Me. They attracted My enmity only because they began to bother you. You see how much I love you and care for you. You will now understand that whatever I will demand of you will be nothing else than an expression of that love.

All this, however, is clearly not included in the *p'shuto shel mikra.*

10 Once more, you can permit yourself a peek into chapter 21 where we tackle this issue, and once more I recommend against it. Let the ideas mature within you as step by hard-won step you struggle on. You will be much the better for it.

11 Of the three, the most significant for our purpose is the middle one: to which covenant does the Ribono shel Olam refer here? In chapter 2 we will find that on this issue Ramban argues with many of the classic commentators. This book is an attempt to draw conclusions from this Ramban concerning the entire thrust of *Ma'amad Har Sinai*. We will be making reference to it in almost every chapter of the book.

12 The term *Mamleches Kohanim VeGoy Kadosh* occurs throughout the book and if you keep your mind open you will find that each mention contributes to a solid understanding of what they mean. See further at chapter 19, note 8, for an attempt to define them more specifically. In addition, you will find some interesting material at the end of the book in the last couple of paragraphs of chapter 21.

TWO *And You Will Be True to My Covenant*

1 See Shemos 19:9 and 20:17 and Devarim 4:10, which all seem to touch upon the point that I am making here. Why was *Ma'amad Har Sinai* necessary? Since each of these references gives different answers, it seems to me that they must be understood as simply pointing out advantages to the particular degree of pomp and circumstance that was attached to the ceremony. Once such a ceremony was necessary, it was done in such and such a way in order to address this and that need. They do not zero in on the essential conundrum. Why was anything at all required?

2 See Rashi to Bereishis 1:31. When the Ribono shel Olam created the world He made everything conditional upon our accepting the Torah.

3 Hence we have the double, שמע תשמעו.

4 ושמרתם את בריתי שאכרות עמכם על שמירת התורה. Nothing could be simpler, or so I thought until today when I happened to glance at Yirmiyahu, chapter 7 (the haftorah for *parashas* Tzav when it is not Shabbos HaGadol). At one point in that chapter the prophet castigates the people for thinking that as long as they conscientiously bring various sacrifices, God will overlook their egregious behavior in other aspects of their lives. The prophet disabuses them. He conveys God's message that reminds them (verses 22–23) that when they left Egypt, He never mentioned anything to them about bringing sacrifices. All he asked of them was שמעו בקולי והייתי לכם לאלהים ואתם תהיו לי לעם, *Listen to My voice and I will be your God and you will be My people.* The prophet points out that God is more interested in holy living than in our sacrificial service.

I asked myself where God had said anything like this when we left Egypt, and it struck me that this quote sounded very much like the verse at *Matan Torah* with which we are dealing, and that, moreover, it sounds very much like Ramban's interpretation. The *bris* is identified as demanding a certain relationship with the Ribono shel Olam (Avraham's *bris*) rather than demanding that we keep the *mitzvos* (the Mishpatim *bris* as defined by the Rashi that we have just quoted).

I checked Rashi to Yirmiyahu and found the following (verse 22):

יום הוציאי אותם תחלת תנאי לא היתה אלא אם שמוע תשמעו בקולי ושמרתם את בריתי והייתם לי סגולה.

Rashi confirms my suspicion. He quotes our very *pasuk* and seems perfectly satisfied with Yirmiyahu's paraphrase. This is so, although, as we have just pointed out, that paraphrase appears to agree with Ramban's rather than his own interpretation. I offer this only as an observation. I do not know enough about Rashi to have a clear idea about how such apparent contradictions ought to be solved or whether, in fact, they call for a solution. Perhaps it is unremarkable that Rashi would have considered different interpretations at different times.

5 והוא הברית שכרת משה עם ישראל אחר מתן תורה בבנותו המזבח. Note, however, that Ibn Ezra disagrees about the timing. In contrast to Rashi he asserts that the placement of that incident is chronologically correct. It happened *after Matan Torah.*

6 הברית אשר כרתי את אבותיכם להיות להם לאלהים ולזרעם אחריהם.

7 והוצאתי, והצלתי, וגאלתי.

8 ולקחתי אתכם לי לעם.

9 At this point, I am using the word מצוה, with a very general meaning. Later in this book we will spend much time demonstrating that *Aseres HaDibros* had significant characteristics and implications beyond their standing as *mitzvos.*

THREE *Beginning to Consolidate Ramban's Interpretation of the* Bris

1 There is another Ramban that fits into this pattern. Ramban comments on Shemos 20:17. There Moshe Rabbeinu explains to the Israelites that they have nothing to fear from having heard the Ribono shel Olam speak to them directly, because God did so only לנסות אתכם. What precisely does this phrase mean? Rashi offers an interpretation but Ramban goes his own way. Here is the Ramban:

ועל דעתי הוא נסיון ממש–יאמר, הנה רצה האלהים לנסותכם התשמרו מצותיו כי הוציא מלבכם כל ספק, ומעתה יראה הישכם אוהבים אותו ואם תחפצו בו . . . שאין לך בריה שאין הקב"ה מנסה אותה, העשיר מנסה אותו אם תהיה ידו פתוחה לעניים, העני מנסה אותו אם יוכל לקבל יסורין וכו' ולכך אמר הכתוב, הטיב לכם האלהים להראותכם את כבודו, אשר לא עשה כן לכל גוי, לנסותכם אם תגמלו לפניו כטובה **אשר עשה עמכם להיות לו לעם נחלה.**

In my opinion, the word is to be translated, in order to test you. God wishes to put you to the test to see whether, now that He has spoken to you and thereby removed any doubts from you, you will keep His commands. He does this because God tests everybody. He tests the wealthy to see whether they will use their riches to treat the poor with an open hand, and He tests the poor to see how much suffering they will bear without anger or bitterness. This, then, is the meaning of this verse: God has showered you with favor by showing you His glory directly, something that He did not do for any other people. This will serve as a test to see whether you will return the favor that He did for you by making you into an *eternal nation to Him*.

Clearly Ramban is consistent with his interpretation of the *bris* at Shemos 19:5.

2 Don't bother counting in our *parshah*. The system that Chazal use to get to the number seven is complex. If you want to follow up on this rather arcane area of Aggadah, you might study Ramban (19:20) who spends some time working out how Chazal arrived at this number. My objective here is not to deal with the esoteric areas upon which all this seems to touch, but simply to explore the possible meaning—of course at the level of *p'shat*—of words that appear in the Torah text.

3 By chance (or perhaps through *hashgachah*) I came across a Ramban that seems absolutely to confirm my suspicion that "Torah," as Ramban uses the word, may well refer specifically to *Aseres HaDibros*. You can find this comment in his glosses on Rambam's Sefer HaMitzvos in the section where Ramban lists the negative commands that, in his opinion, the Rambam omitted but should have included. The second negative command refers to Devarim 4:9–10. In Ramban's view these two verses deal specifically with the Sinaitic experience and *Aseres HaDibros*. Ramban is puzzled since in Kiddushin 30a the Gemara uses these verses to prove that a grandfather is obliged to teach "Torah" to his grandson. But, as Ramban reads the verses, they refer specifically to *Aseres HaDibros* rather than to "Torah" in general. He answers that even though the verses refer specifically to *Aseres HaDibros*, it is still correct to call them "Torah" since למוד אמונת התורה היא הלמוד בתורה.

FOUR *The* Luchos *as "Testimonial" and as "Covenant"*

1 This term is used in order to accommodate those Rishonim who do not count אנכי... as a *mitzvah*.

2 Last Shabbos morning, during Shacharis, it occurred to me that for the first time I had understood the reading in ישמח משה, which makes an issue of the fact that Shabbos is one of those *Dibros* that have their place on the *luchos* and *also* are recorded in the Torah (וכתוב בהם שמירת שבת וכן כתוב בתורתיך). Why is that duality significant? I believe that from what I have just written we have the beginnings of a real answer. The sense of the passage is to point out that Shabbos has the characteristics of both a constitutional principle and a regular *mitzvah*. The implications of this do not belong in this book, but I have the feeling that there is much here that could be developed.

Providentially, I learned Berachos 5a this morning. The Gemara offers the following interpretation of the *pasuk* ואתנה לך את לחות האבן והתורה והמצוה (Shemos 24:12). "לוחות" refers to *Aseres HaDibros*, "תורה" refers to scripture. Once more, although both of course constitute תורה שבכתב, Chazal divide them into different categories. Perhaps the explanation lies in what I have suggested here.

Because I had these issues on my mind, it suddenly occurred to me that we have the same idea expressed in the *parshiyos* that we are studying. In Mishpatim 24:12 the Ribono shel Olam promises Moshe Rabbeinu, "I will give you the stone tablets, the Torah and the *mitzvos*. . . ." The commentators were clearly struck by the wording. We know that the Ribono shel Olam gave Moshe Rabbeinu the tablets on Sinai. In what sense did He also give him "Torah and *mitzvos*"? Rashi explains that we can look upon *Aseres HaDibros* as ten general categories under which all the other *mitzvos* may be subsumed. Ramban, however, appears to learn that these were two separate entities that were given to Moshe Rabbeinu on Mount Sinai. The *luchos* with their *Aseres HaDibros* engraved upon them, and something called "*Torah UMitzvos*," which he does not define further. However, he does make reference to Devarim 5:28, which seems to confirm his thesis. After the Ribono shel Olam had told Moshe Rabbeinu to send the people back to their tents, He said to him "But you stay here with Me and I will speak to you of all the *mitzvos*, *chukim*, and *mishpatim* that you are to teach them. . . ." Once more the "*mitzvos*" that are inscribed upon the *luchos* are treated separately from the other *mitzvos*. Again, the thesis that I have proposed appears to be confirmed.

3 At this point I owe an apology to my good friend, Dr. Richard Steiner. He has written and published an important essay that sets out to prove that the singular form of דברות is דָּבֵר, sometimes appearing as דיבר and sometimes as דביר. I was convinced by his persuasive presentation. [For those interested, the formation of the plural דברות from דָּבֵר would be analogous to כסאות from כִּסֵּא.] I have elected to stay with the probably incorrect דברה in order to spare my readers the added tension of an unfamiliar and somewhat disturbing form. Our subject matter is hard enough as it is.

☞ 4 THIS IS AN EXTREMELY IMPORTANT NOTE AND I WILL BE REFERENCING IT THROUGHOUT THIS BOOK.

The number fourteen is based upon Rambam's Sefer HaMitzvos, as follows:
Negative *Mitzvos*:

1. לא יהיה לך אלהים אחרים על פני
2. לא תעשה [לך] פסל וכל תמונה
5. לא תשתחוה להם
6. ולא תעבדם

Numbers 2, 5, and 6 bring the total count up to thirteen. Then, in the fourth *Dibra* (or perhaps *Dibeir*), we have: Positive Mitzvos: 155, זכור את יום השבת לקדשו, and Negative Mitzvos 320, לא תעשה כל מלאכה. Number 320 brings the total up to fourteen.

Perhaps the most important issue in this book is the differentiation between *mitzvos* and *Dibros*. The assertions that we make here about *Aseres HaDibros* rest upon this distinction. It seeks to answer the very obvious question: If besides being *mitzvos* they are also something else, what precisely is that "something else"? The answer that I suggest is that the ten "*Dibros*" are designed to be the constitutional underpinnings of a nation

that is defined as *Mamleches Kohanim* and *Goy Kadosh*. That is my thesis.
However, there is a complication. As you will see as you go further in this book, much of my thinking is based upon the Ramban's Chumash commentary. Now, Ramban, in his glosses to Sefer HaMitzvos (Negative *Mitzvos* 5) disagrees with Rambam's count and eliminates numbers 2, 5, and 6 from the count. He believes that whatever these three phrases forbid is to be subsumed under the general heading of לא יהיה לך. Accordingly, the assertion that *Aseres HaDibros* contain fourteen *mitzvos* does not hold true according to Ramban.

Does this discovery undermine the entire edifice that I am in the process of erecting?

I think not, and therein lies the significance of this note.

In the first place, Ramban, as far as I can make out, argues with Rambam only in his interpretation of the second *Dibra*. He appears to agree with Rambam that the fourth *Dibra*, Shabbos, contains two *mitzvos*, one positive (זכור...) and one negative (לא תעשה...). If so, the *mitzvah* count of the *Dibros* is still not ten but eleven. So the *mitzvah* count is still not congruent with the *Dibra* count. My essential argument is as strong with a discrepancy of one as it would be with a discrepancy of four.

Even beyond that, if, for argument's sake, it were possible to show that Ramban disagrees with Rambam even on negative command 320 and believes that the number of *mitzvos* is, in fact, congruent with the number of *Dibros*, I would still feel on firm ground in making my argument. It is absolutely clear to me that Ramban agrees with Rambam's definition of a *Dibra*. The issue is so basic that if Ramban would have disagreed with Rambam, he would have left some written evidence of that disagreement. Absent such a written record, I must assume that Ramban agrees with Rambam in this matter.

5 Although the word *eidus* has been used before in connection with the ark (the first time is at Shemos 25:16) Rashi there had learned that reference is to the Sefer Torah that Moshe Rabbeinu was to write at the end of the forty years. See Gur Aryeh there for Rashi's reasoning. Ramban, however, has assumed throughout that the earlier uses of *eidus* also had the *luchos* in mind.

6 I find it interesting that although *Aseres HaDibros* are called both *eidus* and *bris*, and the *aron* is called both *Aron HaBris* and *Aron HaEidus*, we have *Mishkan HaEidus* but not *Mishkan HaBris*.

In addition, I have no explanation for the fact that in Shemos it is always *Luchos HaEidus*, never *Luchos HaBris*, and in Devarim it is the other way around, *Luchos HaBris* but never *Luchos HaEidus*.

7 We deal with this concept expansively in chapter 7.

8 We discuss what might be the underlying value in each of the ten *Dibros* in chapters 9 through 19.

NOTES

FIVE *Rashi on* K'sheih Oref

1. I have borrowed most of this translation from R. Aryeh Kaplan's The Living Torah.
2. Throughout these essays we shall base ourselves upon Maharal in Gur Aryeh on Shemos 32:13 that God's threat—to destroy the people and to begin afresh with Moshe Rabbeinu's family—means just that. The Avos would not be our Avos anymore because the nation that they had built had been rejected. The choice of Moshe Rabbeinu would result in an entirely new beginning, a new nation with a single new patriarch who would be Moshe Rabbeinu.
3. עם קשה עורף. I translated literally. I suppose that the closest English term would be *obstinate*.
4. Dear Reader, I feel that I must share with you a discomfort that I had with Rashi's interpretation of verse 9 and the solution that I found.

   I had thought that verse 10, where the Ribono shel Olam threatens to wipe out the Jewish people and replace them with Moshe Rabbeinu's family, followed on from verse 9. "*They are stiff-necked, therefore I will kill them.*" But as I have understood Rashi, that is not the case. Verse 9 only explains why there is no point in hoping that they will repent. It does not spell out the actual sin for which they had forfeited their right to be considered God's chosen people. That did not seem logical to me.

   However, I noticed that verse 7 where God begins to speak, is introduced by *VaYedaber HaShem*, whereas verse 9 begins with *VaYomer HaShem*.

   Apparently, then, we are dealing with two speeches. As I will work it out, verses 7, 8, and 10 are one speech. Verse 9 stands on its own, as we shall now explain.

   We know that *VaYedaber* without a softening *Leimor* signifies a harsh way of talking, but *VaYomer* signifies a soft, reconciliatory mode of speech.

   Accordingly, it appears to me that God's first speech consists of verses 7, 8, and 10, the dreadful sin that the people had committed and God's decision to destroy them because of that sin.

   Verse 9 is a kind of interjection. It says, more or less, "Don't feel shocked that I express Myself so harshly. Is there not always a chance that they will come to realize how badly they have sinned? The fact is that, in all probability, they will not. They are a stiff-necked people and will not readily back down from what they have done."

   This, of course, does not soften the question that we asked in the body of the essay—the people *did* repent; they *were* forgiven—on Rashi's interpretation. However, it does explain how, in Rashi's mind, the sentences are to be structured.

NOTES

SIX *Ramban on* K'sheih Oref

1 קשה עורף.

2 One of our questions was how the people thought that a figure, only now manufactured from their own jewelry, was going to replace Moshe Rabbeinu. That is a reasonable question and requires a sensible answer. I am not going to address it in these essays because it appears to me from the Ramban that the answer borders upon *sisrei Torah*. The interested reader should consult the Ramban to Shemos 32:1.

3 Of course there was the hint in God's words that Moshe's prayer could help (Rashi to Shemos 32:10), as indeed at the end it did. But it is quite clear that without that prayer things would have turned out as I describe them here.

4 Page 171 in the Chavel edition of the Kisvei HaRamban. We can only bring a small excerpt from this essay, but, if it is possible for you, I would highly recommend a visit there. He discusses and brings source material for the prohibition against seeking intermediaries between ourselves and the Ribono shel Olam beyond anything that we have here.

5 To translate זובח לאלהים יחרם בלתי לה' לבדו, I have used R. Aryeh Kaplan's translation. It is a little loose, but conveys the main idea in the *pasuk* בלתי לה' לבדו precisely.

6 See Ramban, Shemos 20:15–16, that the conversation between Moshe Rabbeinu and the people described in Shemos 20:15–18 took place *before Aseres HaDibros* were given. Ramban explains why the Torah chose to report that conversation *out of place* after *Aseres HaDibros*. It transpires that there was evidently no break at all between *Aseres HaDibros* and the *Atem re'isem*... passage that we are now examining.

7 I have the sense that people who are lucky enough to be in Eretz Yisrael and are willing to stand in line for hours for a couple of minutes' time with our Gedolei Yisrael do so because they realize that, in a real sense, these wonderful people project an image of royalty. I have often wondered why it has become the custom to greet these Gedolim with the song, ימים על ימי מלך תוסיף. I cannot swear to it, but as far as I can remember, there was no such usage many years ago when I was in Yeshivah.

8 Kesubos 17a.

9 There is a strong basis in Chazal that the Ribono shel Olam displays different characteristics at different times. Thus they teach that at Sinai He appeared as a זקן יושב בישיבה while at Yam Suf He projected Himself as a גבור עושה מלחמה.

10 Targum explains that this refers to Beis HaMikdash that we will build for the Ribono shel Olam to dwell among us.

11 Take a peek at the next chapter where I quote R. Shimshon Pincus on the love and caring that was expressed in that sentence.

12 As this idea was germinating in my mind, it occurred to me that it might be able to explain why the first *Dibra*, even according to those Rishonim who

consider it to be a *mitzvah,* was not given in the form of a command. (In chapter 9 note 1 I make an attempt to answer this question by a slightly different route.) When the correct relationship is established, orders become unnecessary. On the wings of love the slightest hint becomes an iron-clad order. In this context it would be useful to brush up our memory of Mesilas Yesharim, chapter 18, in his discussion of *chasidus.*

אמנם מי שאוהב את הבורא ית"ש אהבה אמתית לא ישתדל ויכוין לפטור עצמו במה שכבר מפורסם מן החובה אשר על כל ישראל בכלל, אלא יקרה לו כמו שיקרה אל בן אוהב אביו שאילו יגלה אביו את דעתו גילוי מעט שהוא חפץ בדבר מן הדברים, כבר ירבה הבן בדבר ההוא ובמעשה ההוא כל מה שיוכל. ואע"פ שלא אמרו אביו אלא פעם אחת ובחצי דיבור, הנה די לאותו הבן להבין היכן דעתו של אביו נוטה לעשות לו, גם את אשר לא אמר לו בפירוש, כיון שיוכל לדון בעצמו שיהיה הדבר ההוא נחת רוח לפניו ולא ימתין שיצוהו יותר בפירוש או שיאמר לו פעם אחרת.

However, someone who truly loves the Ribono shel Olam will not consider that he has fulfilled his duty once he has done what is specifically demanded by the law. He would go beyond the requirements of the law just like a son who loves his father, for whom even a small hint that his father might want something is enough to spur him to act to the fullest extent of his ability. He would do his utmost even though his father had only indicated a certain wish in general terms, because from the little that his father had said he could work all the details out for himself. He has no need to wait for the father to spell out what he ought to do, and would never wait for his father to make his request a second time.

When we think about it, it becomes clear that the unexpected form that this first Dibra takes is analogous to the first verse of Kri'as Shema. That verse, too, is counted as a mitzvah, the mitzvah of קבלת עול מלכות שמים, and we are halachically required to accept that yoke each time that we recite Kri'as Shema. Once more, at the most basic belief that the Torah requires of us, we are expected to take a hint rather than have our obligations spelled out to us. We have detected a significant pattern here.

SEVEN Matan Torah—*God's Wedding Day*

1 Ramban's language in his comment to 19:4 seems to me to make it quite clear that the Ribono shel Olam's presence on the mountain preceded our coming to Sinai. On להביא אתכם אלי, *to bring you unto Me,* he remarks, *to the place where My glory rested, this mountain where My* SHECHINAH *is to be found.* It strikes me that this is reminiscent of our custom to have the Chasan enter the Chupah first and to have the Kallah come to him. The Chasan joyously anticipated the approach of his Kallah.

2 Rashi, Ta'anis 26b takes אמו (literally, *his mother*) as כנסת ישראל.

3 Reference is to Yom Kippur, the day upon which we received the second *luchos* (Rashi, Ta'anis 26b). Throughout these essays I assume that the sixth or seventh of Sivan, the day when the Ribono shel Olam communicated

Aseres HaDibros to us, is also included in the dictum of Chazal that the day of "*Matan Torah*" is considered the day of the Ribono shel Olam's Chasunah. Of course the official date is the day on which the ring—in this case, the *luchos*—was actually handed over. That, as a result of the *Cheit HaEigel*, had to wait till Yom Kippur. However, that which gave the *luchos* their unique status was the text engraved upon them—*Aseres HaDibros*. Once we understand this, it is clear that the process began with God's revelation at Sinai.

4 I offer a paraphrase of the essentials, not of the details. The examples that I use are not his, and the tone of the piece is suited to my small book written in the vernacular, not to his *sefer*.

5 איכפתיות. I do not think that any English phrase can quite catch the true meaning of this wonderful word. I will not even try.

6 Try to translate הוציאו אתי מן הכלים!

7 כביכול, כביכול, עד לשגעון.

8 See Rashi on אתם ראיתם. His comment runs along similar lines.

EIGHT Aseres Hadibros

1 Of course "Dibros" does not occur in Chumash. There we always have *Aseres HaDevarim*. For our purpose, at this stage of our research there is no difference between the two since both are legitimate forms of דבר. That Chazal chose to use an expression that was in general use at the time (it abounds in the halachic Midrashim although in Shas it occurs only in relation to the Decalogue) rather than the Torah term for the same concept need not surprise us.

My good friend, Dr. Richard Steiner, showed me Chullin 137b where Isi bar Hini challenged R. Yochanan who, in teaching his son, used *recheilim* for the plural of *rachel*, sheep, since that is attested in the Torah. Isi argued that nonetheless he should have used *Recheilos*, since לשון תורה לעצמה לשון חכמים לעצמן. Apparently it is not only permitted to Chazal to use their own expressions, it is actually to be preferred.

[It occurred to me to wonder why. I think that intuitively we would have supposed that the Torah language is more sacred and therefore, at least in the context of תלמוד תורה, to be preferred. Upon studying the language that the Gemara uses, I was struck by a peculiarity. The Gemara uses **לעצמן** with לשון חכמים, rather than **לעצמה** as I would have expected. I had thought that this aphorism was to be understood as saying that both languages are, within their own terms (לעצמה), legitimate. If that were the meaning this would have been conveyed by לעצמה. However, לעצמן refers not to the language but to the חכמים. The meaning appears to be that, for the Sages themselves, that which to them comes most naturally is to be preferred. For profound understanding, formal pedantry is to be avoided.

I wonder whether this insight has any relevance to the question whether in English-speaking countries, use of the vernacular ought to be preferred to instruction in Yiddish. Of course I realize that in such a major decision other considerations may also come into play and tip the scales in favor of Yiddish.]

2 ....ידבר נא עבדך דבר

3 ....כל הדבר הקשה

4 See note 4 in chapter 4.

5 In Hebrew these are known as טעמי המקרא or simply טעמים. Popularly they are referred to by the Yiddish, *trope*. There are disjunctive טעמים, the function of which is to divide a sentence or phrase into smaller units, and conjunctive ones, which serve to join words logically and meaningfully within the sentence or phrase. The טעמים are of exegetical value because the meaning of many verses can change radically depending where the breaks are made. The classical TaNaCh commentators certainly take note of the *trope* in their efforts to unravel the meaning of complicated texts. However, they seem not to have considered themselves bound by בעלי הטעמים. They will occasionally consider a different interpretation closer to the truth as they perceive it than the meaning that is yielded by the *trope*.

6 I say, in general terms, because the Torah's treatment of the first two *Dibros* complicates matters considerably. From the third *Dibra,* לא תשא onward, everything flows logically. The fourth *Dibra,* Shabbos, takes up four sentences in the *Ta'am Tachton (pesukim)* but is converted into one long verse in the *Ta'am Elyon (Dibros)* (in this case, one *Dibra* = four *pesukim*). *Dibros* 6, 7, 8, and 9, all very short, are one sentence in the *Ta'am Tachton,* but turn into four discrete *Dibros* in the *Ta'am Elyon* (in that case, one *pasuk* = four *Dibros*). However, the same consistent system does not hold true for the first two *Dibros*. The *Ta'am Tachton* is not problematic. The first *Dibra* takes just one *pasuk* and the second takes three. The *Ta'am Elyon,* however, instead of dividing the two *Dibros* from each other, combines them (according to the *minhag* that uses a רביע for "*avadim,*" the last word of the first *Dibra*). Perhaps the logic behind this irregularity would be that since these two *Dibros,* both uttered by the Ribono shel Olam Himself, are worded in the first person, it made sense to בעלי הטעמים to combine them. See further in the next note.

7 See previous note. Besides the two *te'amim* systems, *Elyon* and *Tachton*, there is also a third consideration that complicates matters considerably. *Aseres HaDibros* are written in the Torah in such a way that in most cases each *Dibra* is a separate *parshah*. Instead of my describing the rather complicated system in this note, I suggest you take a glance in a Tikkun and everything will become very clear. However, there are two totally unexpected exceptions to this usage. *Dibros* 1 and 2 are one *parshah,* but Dibur 10, לא תחמד, is divided into two *parshiyos*.

An analysis lies outside the scope of this book. If you have the chance, I would advise you to read Dr. Mordechai Breuer's detailed treatment titled אנכי ולא יהיה לך מפי הגבורה שמענום, printed in the second volume of his פרקי מועדות. I owe a great deal to his clear and incisive presentation of the subject.

8 It is for this reason that according to the old מנהג אשכנז, the טעם עליון is used only on Shavuos when the *Dibros* are read as *Dibros*. In Yisro and in VaEschanan the טעם תחתון is used.

9 When I say "to work out exactly," I do not mean that I can prove that whatever value I assign in chapters 9 through 19 is in fact *the* message that makes this particular *mitzvah* into a *Dibra*. Clearly there are no proofs. I use the word *exactly* to convey the idea that I will attempt to be as precise as possible in delineating the particular value that I will suggest. None of them are more than suggestions.

10 Rashi's remarks to the Shir HaShirim verse appear to negate what I have said here. On יום חתונתו he writes, יום מתן תורה שעטרוהו להם למלך וקבלו עולו, *The day when the Torah was given, on which they crowned Him as king and accepted His yoke upon themselves.* Rav Pincus's insistence upon the uniqueness of a marital relationship in contrast to a set of legal obligations seems contradicted by this Rashi which speaks about a royal yoke rather than a husband's embrace. At this point I do not know a source for Rashi for weaving the concept "king" into a concept of marriage.

This Rashi really bothers me very much. Rav Pincus's ideas seem to me to be so real and so true that I would truly want to understand Rashi's insistence on involving the Ribono shel Olam's kingship, His character of being a lawgiver, when the concept of Chasunah so clearly seems to belong to the sphere of love and caring.

A glimmer of an answer has occurred to me. Rosh HaShanah 31a discusses the connection between the seven days of the week and the *shir shel yom* that was associated with each day. ה' מלך גאות לבש was to be said on Friday, because on that day, שגמר מעשיו ומלך עליהם. Maharal explains: Kingship is a concept that can exist only within a group in which there is some equality among the members who make up the group. You can talk about the lion being "king" over the animals, because he too is an animal. One animal is king over other animals. However, you cannot speak of the zookeeper being "king" over them. He controls them (משל) but does not rule (מלך) over them. God was a משל until He created Adam since nothing else in the created world as it was before Adam was created had any affinity to Him. Only after man had been created בצלם was God able to become a "king."

The relationship (indicated by the "ה" in יום הששי, see Rashi there) between the sixth day of Creation and the sixth day of Sivan (*Matan Torah*) was, in the first place, that the Kingship which the Ribono shel Olam had exercised over individual men up until then now would begin to express itself in full bloom over a Godly nation.

The Torah refers to a married woman as one who is בית אִישָׁהּ, as having entered her husband's house (אם בית אישה נדרה). Naomi used the same expression when she was attempting to persuade her daughters-in-law to return home. What happens when you marry a king, whose home is a palace? It turns out that your home is, in fact, complex, consisting of two very different units. There is the warm and cozy home of the loving husband, and there is the formal palace of the king governed by all manner of stiffness and protocols. Neither is truer than the other. Both contribute to a complex reality.

Rashi in Shir HaShirim could indeed have chosen to speak of the warmer, softer aspect of marriage. But, under the influence of the Chazal that he quoted in his Bereishis commentary, and aware that in cosmic terms the establishment of God's kingship was presumably the more significant of the two, he chose as he chose.

It is worthwhile noting that we have a similar situation in respect to Shabbos. On the one hand we welcome the Shabbos on Friday night by greeting her as a Kallah, באי כלה באי כלה, and on the other hand there are many sources that treat Shabbos as either king (מלכא) or queen (מלכתא). There are even those who have the custom of ending לכה דודי with the words, באי כלה באי כלה שבת מלכתא.

11 The translation of the excerpt from the Shabbos Minchah *Shemoneh Esrei* is based on the ArtScroll rendering.

12 This is Yiddish for *a suitable match*. Please take the time to look at the second half of the Preface. It adds clarity to what I have written here.

NINE *The First* Dibra

1 I have not seen anyone attempting to explain what purpose is served by wording a command as a simple statement, essentially as a non-command. See chapter 6, note 12.

I think that the following will help to explain. In the Gemara we sometimes find the question, למה לי קרא, סברא היא? *Why does the Torah require a* PASUK *to teach us a given fact? Is it not self-evident on the basis of simple logic?* Clearly there is an assumption that the Torah relies on us to think logically and correctly. It will normally not put something into writing that, with a little thought, is self-evident.

It seems to me that after the Ribono shel Olam Himself announces that it is He and no one else Who brought us out of Egypt, it would follow logically that we are obliged to believe in that fact and in all the consequences that follow from it, for example that we ought to accept His kingship over us.

By wording this most fundamental of principles in a statement and leaving it to us to work out the consequences by using our own healthy intellect, the Ribono shel Olam was teaching us a vastly significant lesson. We were about to receive the beginnings of what was ultimately to become our Torah. The Ribono shel Olam needed to teach us that, in interpreting it, we are to freely use our minds. Through the medium of *Torah shebe'al peh,* we are to become partners with the Ribono shel Olam in producing Torah.

2 האמנת האלהות.

3 The Hebrew אמונה carries complex connotations, which make it difficult to translate into another language. In the present context, "belief" will do as long as we realize that it is not *the* definitive rendering.

4 Rambam derives the obligation of קבלת מלכות שמים from שמע ישראל which is the second of his Positive Mitzvos. Since Ramban is silent concerning Rambam's second Positive Mitzvah, it seems that he agrees with Rambam's formulation. Why would we require two *mitzvos* to command us to accept heaven's yoke? Perhaps we might postulate that there are two distinct paths by which we can conclude that we are absolutely subordinate to the Ribono shel Olam. The first could be when that realization comes to us by way of contemplation of God's mastery over history (the first *Dibra*). The second path brings us to the same realization by way of contemplation of God's singularity (*Yichud*). It is perhaps incumbent upon us to travel both routes.

5 Ramban's actual language is .קבלת מלכותו, כלומר באמונת האלהות [Please note that this is Rav Chavel's reading. He notes that other editions have אמונת האלהות without the "ב" prefix. It makes a difference.] For those of you who want to take this further, it seems to me that there is rich potential here for careful analysis. However, it falls outside the scope of this essay.

6 Please do not ascribe any significance to the switch from "slave" to "servant." The term "slave" carries negative connotations in common usage and somehow seemed to me inappropriate when describing our relationship to the Ribono shel Olam.

7 .שטרי קודם

8 .עבד מלך כמלך

9 Chazal refer to prayer as **עבודה** שבלב. I understand the Rabbeinu Yonah as follows. At a superficial level we might well ask why asking the Ribono shel Olam, as we do in our תפילה, to fulfill all our needs, should be considered an act of service. As Rabbeinu Yonah explains it, the answer lies close at hand. When a cleaning lady asks the person who hired her for a mop, that asking is itself an act of servitude. When we present our requests to the Ribono shel Olam under the impression of the גאולה that made us all His servants, then the requests that we make in our תפילה are no more than a mark of our .עבדות

TEN *The Second* Dibra

1 See Sanhedrin 102b for the story of Menasheh and Rav Ashi.

2 .למינו

3 See Ramban, VaYikra 19:19, that the Torah forbade the grafting of different plants and animals together (כלאים) in order to preserve the מינים, upon which the Ribono shel Olam had insisted at the time of Creation, in their pristine purity.

4 In המצוות השקולות, the last work that the Mashgiach published. According to R. Yonasan David's מכתב ברכה, this book contains the distilled wisdom accumulated during a lifetime of ceaseless labor. It is a gift to us from a master teacher who knew us well and spent a lifetime trying to help us become better.

5 ערך עליון in R. Wolbe's language.

6 Do not make a graven image for yourselves. Do not prostrate yourselves before them. Do not serve them.

7 I suspect that our custom to strike ourselves on the heart when we say חטאנו and פשענו in the sixth *berachah* of the שמונה עשרה derives from this insistence that our feelings be somehow, at least symbolically, translated into some physical reaction.

I recall seeing in a שיעור דעת from one of the Roshei Yeshivah of Telz, an example from everyday life, which illustrates our psychological dependence upon the physical. He notes that we may only just have looked at our watch in order to ascertain the time, when somebody asks us what the time is. Although we have the information clearly in our heads, the tendency is to look at the watch once more. We prefer to have our senses confirm our theoretical knowledge.

8 I knew a house painter who stubbornly refused to put up a WET PAINT sign when he worked. Predictably, people's jackets turned green. He explained that, if there were a sign, everybody would thumb his paint job, to check whether it was indeed still wet. His artistry would be ruined. Nobody would feel the paint because they suspected him of being a liar. It was simply a matter of nature taking over.

9 A large part of this rendering is borrowed from Rabbi Dov Lederman's translation of the Kuzari (Jerusalem: Kalman Steinberg, 2000).

10 This translation is taken from *The Living Torah* by the late R. Aryeh Kaplan.

11 I believe that a careful reading of the Ramban on this verse confirms what I am about to suggest.

12 I wonder whether it might be permitted to play a recording of thunder, and shofar blasts in order to create an atmosphere conducive to כונה during *davening*. Something tells me that even if it were halachically permitted, it would still be frowned upon.

ELEVEN *The Third* Dibra

1 The exact way in which the Ribono shel Olam is invoked when a *shevu'ah* is made will be discussed further along in this essay.

2 See VaYikra 19:12.

3 Shevu'os 39a implies that the prohibition against making a false oath is also somehow included in our *Dibra*. There we learn that before Beis Din permitted one of the litigants to take an oath affirming his claim, they warned him as to the seriousness of swearing falsely. One of the warnings centered upon our *Dibra*. They told him that when this *Dibra* was announced, the entire world trembled in fear. Now, Beis Din was obviously concerned that the litigant might be tempted to swear *falsely*. If they still invoked our *Dibra*, this indicates that false oaths are also somehow covered here.

4 כי לא ינקה.

5 There are different opinions among the Rishonim whether God's name must actually be mentioned as a part of the *shevu'ah* formula. For the pur-

pose of this essay, there is no need to take a position on this issue. It is clear that even if an actual mention is not required, God's presence is still very real within the *shevu'ah* context.

6 It seems likely that Radbaz was thinking of the Rambam, Yesodei HaTorah 1:3, אין אמתתו כאמתת אחד מהם.

7 The extremely stringent position of the Radbaz does not seem to be universally accepted. Thus Sefer HaChinuch writes that the person who swears to shoulder a given action is obliged to abide by that obligation eternally, *in precisely the same way that God Himself is eternal* and not subject to any change. A similar statement can be found in Ibn Ezra to Shemos 20:7 where he writes, *The reason for mentioning the Divine name is to imply that just as He that goes by that name is true, so are the words of him who is swearing, true.*
I venture to guess that both the Sefer HaChinuch and Ibn Ezra would agree to Rambam's assertion concerning God's singularity (see note 6). The reason why they do not share Radbaz's abhorrence of this formulation is because they read the meaning of the comparison differently than does Radbaz. If, indeed, the person who is taking the oath would mean an absolute parity between the two "truths," Radbaz's objections would undeniably be correct. However, it is possible to read the words differently. The person means only that his commitment is total and will not change just as the Ribono shel Olam will never change. He is not at all entering into the philosophical question of what the idea "truth" means when applied to the Ribono shel Olam.

8 I have always wondered why our Shulchan Aruch begins with the seemingly trivial issues of how we are supposed to get dressed in the morning. One would have supposed that the question of whether or not the right shoe goes on first in the morning is an issue of no great moment.
Perhaps it is this very question that persuaded the Ramo to insert שויתי ה' לנגדי תמיד at the beginning of these *halachos*. When we are in the presence of the Ribono shel Olam, there are no matters of small moment. The matter of the sequence of the shoes becomes a חמורה שבחמורות.

TWELVE *The Fourth* Dibra

1 Actually, that is not quite accurate. We associate Kiddush with a particular wording and with a cup of wine. Neither of these is necessary under Torah law. Nevertheless, I am leaving the sentence as it stands, because in practical terms that is exactly what we do.

2 Our *Dibra* contains another *mitzvah,* besides the one that we are discussing. It is, לא תעשה כל מלאכה, the prohibition against working on Shabbos (Negative Commands 320 in Rambam's Sefer HaMitzvos). For our purposes in this book, we will leave that *mitzvah* unexplored. It is as I wrote at the beginning of this essay. For that aspect of the Shabbos there is so much material available that I really believe that I have nothing much to add.

3 As are, for example, the prohibition of walking outside the *Techum* (Negative

Mitzvos 321) and the obligation to rest on Shabbos (Positive Mitzvos 154). These are perfectly good *mitzvos* but do not, apparently, rise to the level of *Dibros*.

4 The entire verse, but most of all the final words, אשר ברא אלהים לעשות, is difficult to translate. The exact rendering does not affect our argument in this essay. I have chosen to follow R. Samson Rafael Hirsch's translation.

5 As in everything else that deals with Shabbos, there are profound depths to every single detail. The interested reader may want to study Ma'amar 7 in Rav Hutner's Pachad Yitzchak on Shabbos.

6 I have a sense that this Ibn Ezra has found its way into the vernacular. I believe that when our wonderful wives are cooking and cleaning for Shabbos, they say that they are "making" Shabbos.

7 If you have R. Yehudah Copperman's S'forno with his footnotes, it would pay to consult it at this point. He explains the language and references a different S'forno (Shemos 16:29) where he makes the same point.

8 Actually we could even ask ourselves that same question, in the earlier part of the evening while we are still in Shul singing באי כלה באי כלה, inviting the bride into our homes. If the place where we live is a spiritual hovel, the Kallah may not be interested in accepting the invitation.

THIRTEEN *The Fifth* Dibra

1 My dictionary tells me that it came into use in 1947.

2 It is constantly reiterated that the counting was done למשפחותם לבית אבותם.

3 This rendering is a paraphrase rather than a translation.

4 For the argument that concerns us here, the details of all these ideas are not important. See below, note 8.

5 Rashi to BeMidbar 1:18. **ויתילדו** הביאו ספרי יוחסיהם ועדי חזקת לידתם כל אחד ואחד להתיחס על השבט.

6 בשעה שקבלו ישראל את התורה נתקנאו אומות העולם בהן. מה ראו להתקרב יותר מן האומות. סתם פיהם הקב"ה. אמר להן הביאו לי ספר יוחסין שלכם.

7 I have paraphrased this Rambam rather than offering a literal translation.

8 See note 4. Maharal explains the necessity of the coercive element in *Matan Torah*. See, for example, Gur Aryeh to Shemos 19:17.

9 למשפחותם לבית אבתם.

10 I followed R. Aryeh Kaplan's translation of this passage.

11 See Rav Dessler's Michtav MeiEliyahu, vol. 3, p. 361.

12 See Mishnah, Sotah 9:15. Shortly before Moshiach will come . . . youngsters will shame their elders, elders will rise before youth, sons will treat their fathers disdainfully, and daughters will rebel against their mothers.

13 For practical purposes, I believe that the Torah's proposal for a fail-safe method of perpetuating the *mesorah* is still very much in order. "Sons" and "grandsons" can, in the Torah's system, stand just as well for *talmidim*. Our *mesorah* and our future are still in good hands. It is the unbounded privilege

of our generation to have witnessed how the Yeshivos have been able to step in, *in loco parentis,* where this is necessary.

14 I am indebted for these references to Taryag Mitzvos HaShalem under the editorship of Rabbi David Wachs.

FOURTEEN *The Sixth* Dibra *I*

1 Before the *mabul* Adam had been granted only the vegetable world as food (see Bereishis 1:29). After the *mabul* the Ribono shel Olam permitted him to consume meat (See Ramban, VaYikra 17:11). Ramban, there, discusses why this change came about. In the present context we do not need to deal with that issue.

2 שפך דם האדם באדם דמו ישפך כי בצלם אלהים עשה את האדם.

3 The expression, *in the image of God,* describes that uniqueness.

4 I could not resist a peek into my *Chicago Manual of Style* and found this rather stuffy remark: Phrases such as *very unique, more unique, somewhat unique* and so on, in which a degree is attributed to *unique,* are poor usage. So now it is official.

5 The phrase about God having used the Torah as a blueprint for creating the world is not included in the text of all Siddurim. However, it is included in the standard Mishnayos and the standard commentators (including the Gra) had it in their reading. Because of this I feel confident in using the phrase for the purpose of developing my argument.

6 Yes, I know that there is no such transitive verb. Well, now there is. To me, at least, it rings true.

7 Here is a short quote from Rav Wolbe in his אדם ביקר, page 47.

אך גדר האדם מצד העבודה שלו הוא, שהוא בעל גוף, וזאת היא עבודתו לקדש ולטהר ולרומם את הגוף, **שיהיה הוא ראוי לקום בתחית המתים** ליאור באור החיים הנצחיים.

If we seek to define man in the context of the service that is demanded of him, the premise upon which all else is based is the fact that he is a physical entity, he has a body. The purpose of the service that he is required to perform for the Ribono shel Olam is to imbue the physical with sanctity, to purify it and to uplift it to the state in which it will deserve to be resurrected at *Techiyas HaMeisim* with the goal that at that time it will be able to bask in the eternal light.

8 My sense is that this phrase has made its way into the public domain and can therefore be used without crediting. In any case, I am using the concept in a sense that is diametrically opposite of the way it was used by the originators.

FIFTEEN *The Sixth* Dibra *II*

1 In halachic terms, this assumption is confirmed by Maccos 6a. The *sugia* is dealing with the principle, עדות שבטלה מקצתה בטלה כולה, that the presence of

one disqualified witness renders the entire group of which he is a part invalid. The Gemara asks that, if so, it should never be possible to carry out a death sentence against the murderer. Since the victim himself is an interested party, and therefore disqualified from giving evidence, he automatically disqualifies any other witnesses who may have seen the crime. The Gemara accepts this cavil [temporarily] and rules that, indeed, the death penalty would only be possible if the killer murdered his victim from behind where his victim was unable to see him.

The entire *sugia* makes clear that the victim has standing as an interested party who has a legal stake in the punishment that is to be meted out to the murderer.

2 In fact, of course, any transgression of civil law is not only an offense against the person who was damaged by our actions, but also against the Ribono shel Olam Whose law we flouted by harming our fellow. However, what Ramban stresses here is qualitatively different from such cases. When I break my neighbor's window I am not breaking God's window. I offend against my victim by inflicting fiscal damage upon him and I offend against God by disobeying His command. Those are two very different things. We might word the difference by describing my neighbor's loss as direct and the Ribono shel Olam's loss as indirect.

However, Ramban here is dealing with a totally different dimension. The life that the murderer took was precious to two parties. His crime was a direct attack upon two equally bereft victims. His action denied his victim the use of his life and it denied the Ribono shel Olam the satisfaction of having Himself extolled by this individual in a manner that only his unique mix of qualities could have produced. It is not a matter of having the Ribono shel Olam's laws flouted. That is also true, but no truer than it is in any civil case. Here the Ribono shel Olam is a sufferer at a level that equals that of the victim.

3 If we are going to be citizens of a *Mamleches Kohanim VeGoy Kadosh,* we must will ourselves to live within the culture that must permeate such a kingdom and such a nation. If our neighbor, Reuven, is just that to us, good old Reuven with whom I went to school and played stickball when we were small, then we have failed miserably and utterly in the challenge that the Ribono shel Olam laid down for us when, so long ago, we stood at Sinai.

As I am writing this endnote, I am sitting at home in my study where one of the pictures on the wall is that of R. Moshe Schwab זצ"ל, *mashgiach* of the Gateshead Yeshiva all those many years ago. I remember well that in his many unforgettable *schmuesen* he often quoted his *mashgiach* in the pre-war Mirrer Yeshivah. As R. Moshe would tell it, R. Yerucham זצ"ל once saw a horse pulling a cart down the street of tiny (but "enormous" and immortal) Mir. He asked his students what they saw. Bewildered, they answered "*A Wogen mit a Pferd,*" a wagon and a horse. R. Yerucham corrected them: "*Dos is a Wogen? Dos is a Pferd?! Dos is rotzon HaShem wos geyt in der Gass!*" "Do you really think that that is all that you are seeing?! Are you hung up on the cart and the horse?! What you are really seeing is God's will unfolding in the guise of a horse and cart moving down the street!"

I am not sure what all this meant to me as a sixteen year old. I think that in the context of what I have now written about a *Mamleches Kohanim VeGoy Kadosh*, I understand it better.

4 I have used R. Chavel's translation.

5 I suppose that this means in the sense of being the *original cause.*

6 I suppose that this means in the sense of being the *immediate cause.*

7 Of course it is possible that somewhere, in Ramban's vast literary output, there is some discussion of this issue; perhaps he even writes somewhere that, in fact, gratitude plays a significant role in this *mitzvah*. I just do not know. However, I have looked in the obvious places and have not come across it.

SIXTEEN *The Seventh* Dibra

1 I have made use of Rav Chavel's translation in this passage.

2 I do not know how to deal with this Ramban. If I am reading him correctly —and after intense scrutiny I see no other way—he is maintaining that the honor due to the adulterer (no less!) will, by mistake, be paid to the cuckolded husband of the woman. The child will not know that he is not the child of the husband and nevertheless will treat him, a total stranger, with the respect due to a father.

But how can Ramban claim that the child would be legally bound to honor his biological father who is an adulterer? It is well-known throughout Shas that honor is only due to someone classified as עושה מעשה עמך, and that is certainly not the case in our situation. Perhaps Ramban is thinking of a case in which the adulterer subsequently did *teshuvah*. Since Ramban mentions none of this, I would be inclined to assume that I have made a mistake in my reading of Ramban. However, in all honesty, I cannot see where I have erred.

I discussed the issue with my good friend, Rabbi Hillel Danziger, the editorial director of the ArtScroll Ramban, and he suggested that the Ramban may not be speaking about a single act of adultery but describing a society within which adultery is rife. In such a society all kinds of mix-ups could occur. If that were the correct reading of the Ramban it would alleviate our problem considerably.

3 I wrote this sentence in the excitement of the moment, but once it was safely on the computer, I had the good sense to check myself. I borrowed a copy of HaRav Simchah Zisel Broyde's ושם דרך on the Ramban and found that he, with what appeared to me to be an equal degree of excitement, made essentially the same discoveries as I am about to unfold before you. Still, אין בית המדרש בלא חדוש, and I will make a few points that do not appear there.

Anyway, I suspect that there must be any number of you readers who are willing to plow through a book written in English, but who may not have seen the relevant passage in the ושם דרך. So for you, it is all new!

4 Please see notes 5 and 6 in chapter 15 for my understanding of the terms "first" and "last" in this context.

5 The theory that I am suggesting could have practical ramifications. The *halachah* (Yoreh De'ah 240:19) permits parents to forgo their right to be served by their children. That stands to reason. The *halachah* grants me a right, and it lies in the nature of a right that it need not be exercised. If I can forgive a debt of money that is owed to me, there is no reason to deny me the right to forgive my claim to service or other considerations. If, however, I am correct in my argument that the non-conventional obligations that Ramban derives from the text are incumbent upon the son and daughter not for their parents' needs but for their own, then these would of course not be subject to the parents' forgiveness.
Of course it is not my purpose to issue any kind of halachic ruling. In this essay my only interest is in the theory.

SEVENTEEN *The Eighth* Dibra

1 In the preparation for this essay I was aided greatly by the volume on *Aseres HaDibros* that is a part of R. Dovid Wax's Sefer TaRYaG Mitzvos HaShalem. I found this thorough compilation most helpful.

2 The outlines of the *halachah* as it applies to *goneiv nefesh* can be found in רמב"ם, הלכות גנבה, פרק ט.

3 עבד עברי is a unique status that has no bearing on the issue at hand. In the first place none of the conditions under which it is possible for an עבד עברי to be sold or acquired apply in our case and, moreover, an עבד עברי, even under circumstances that the *halachah* recognizes, is not "owned" in the sense that we are using the word here. Most ראשונים take the phrase עבד עברי גופו קנוי to refer to the קנין איסור that permits him to live with a שפחה כנענית.

4 See Rashi, Bava Kama 68b: **גניבה בנפש** הגונב נפש ומכרו אין כאן יאוש שאין אדם מתייאש על עצמו **ורחמנא חייביה אע"ג דלא אהנו מעשיו**.

5 See Rashi Gittin 39a:
בשלמא בעבד איכא למימר סתמיה לדמים קאי וה"ק הרי הוא קדוש לימכר אבל בעצמו מי איכא למימר שיהא קדוש לימכר **וכי יש דמים לבן חורין ומה מכירה יש בו** . . .

6 The example that the Gemara uses, taking the victim and standing him up to block the wind from discomfiting the perpetrator, is a particularly pernicious use of the victim. In practical purposes he is converting a human being into a screen.

EIGHTEEN *The Ninth* Dibra

1 A word is in order in explanation of my translation. An endnote is not the place to present a detailed argument that could go on for several pages.

However, for those of you who have read the Hebrew and feel that my rendering presents it incorrectly, I offer the following observations.

The correct understanding of this passage is a matter of translation and punctuation. Since our texts do not provide punctuation marks, we are apt to make mistakes unless we tread very carefully.

The critical words are the following: לומר כי לאלהים לעשות משפט בין יצוריו **כי על כן** בראם להיות ביניהם יושר וצדק. I have underlined כי על כן because that is a very tricky phrase. I assume that many of you readers would, as I have done for many years, intuitively translate this phrase, *Because* (כי) *it was with this purpose in mind* (על כן) *that God created them* (בראם). If this were the correct translation, we would place a comma after יצוריו and that would be that.

However, even before we examine the linguistics, we must admit that this translation cannot possibly be true. What is the "Because . . . " setting out to explain? Let us remember that Ramban had made a statement that asserts that it is God's personal duty to judge people; He did not give this power to us. Given the translation that we offered, that which follows the "Because" would have to justify this claim. But does it? Why should the fact that it had been God's purpose that Jewish society should be one that functions in an aura of fairness and justice require that God Himself, not any humans, should be the judges? Why not trust our *Dayanim* to do a conscientious and efficient job? According to this translation, the logic would be faulty.

What is the correct translation of כי על כן? Till now we translated literally, *Because it was with this purpose in mind*. However, a glance at Bereishis 18:5, כי על כן עברתם על עבדכם will show that the phrase ought not to be taken literally; it is an idiomatic expression for *since*. The meaning is, *since this or that has occurred*. (Rashbam, there, explains this unusual use of the words by postulating that the phrase leaves out the word, אשר. Thus, כי על כן **אשר** . . . , *that which happened came about for the following reason* . . .).

The text that we quoted at the beginning of this endnote must be punctuated as follows: לומר כי לאלהים לעשות משפט בין יצוריו, **כי על כן בראם**, להיות ביניהם יושר וצדק, with two commas setting off the phrase כי על כן בראם. The words immediately preceding this phrase and immediately following upon it, are one thought as follows, . . . כי לאלהים לעשות משפט בין יצוריו להיות ביניהם יושר וצדק. This reading of the Ramban is confirmed by Beis HaYayin, the recently published Ramban commentary.

The thought expressed in the Ramban is as follows: Since God created us, it is His obligation to judge us (in order that fairness and justice should prevail). We will examine the logic behind that statement in the essay.

2 I could, and perhaps should, have cited Ramban to Shemos 21:6 where he states, more forcefully and in more detail than he does here, that God is directly involved in the verdict that judges deliver. Here is a small sampling, once more taken from R. Chavel's translation: *And so did Moses say, For the judgment is God's*; so also did Yehoshafat say, *For you judge not for man, but for the Eternal, and* HE IS WITH YOU IN GIVING JUDGMENT. Similarly scripture says, *God stands in the congregation of God, in the midst of Elohim*

(the judges) HE JUDGES. That is to say in the midst of the congregation of judges He judges, for *it is God Who is the Judge.* And so also it says, *Then both men between whom the controversy is shall* STAND BEFORE HASHEM. And this is the purport of the verse, *For* I WILL NOT JUSTIFY THE WICKED. Clearly the point is made, and there is no doubt about what Ramban means.

I chose the shorter, less detailed Ramban from Devarim for a very good reason. It is that in the Devarim comment he does not simply state the facts but, most important for our needs in this essay, assigns a reason. He explains *why* it is that God is so intimately involved in the court proceedings and it is that which is important to us in the present context.

3 In practice this does not mean that any group of people can simply form a *tzibur* and bring a *korban tzibur.* In the context of *korbanos, "tzibur"* usually means only the entire Jewish community.

4 In II Shmuel, chapter 24, we have the story of the tragic mistake that Dovid HaMelech made in ordering an unauthorized census to be carried out. From the text it is difficult to determine what exactly was wrong, and commentators suggest all kinds of possibilities. Ramban (BeMidbar 1:3) suggests that Dovid did not limit the census to those who were over twenty. He wanted everybody, from *bar mitzvah* upward, to be included. In effect, this means that instead of having only a segment of the people counted (which would have been permitted), he wanted to count "all" of them (which is forbidden).

Ramban explains why counting the whole nation is disallowed. שאין הקב"ה חפץ שיהיו כל ישראל בגדר מנין, *because the Ribono shel Olam does not want that the entirety of the nation be defined by the number of the individuals who are comprised by it.*

Ramban does not explain why attaching a number to the whole nation is distasteful to the Ribono shel Olam. I believe that what we have now learned within can explain. Any plural number defines the unit in relation to what came before and what lies ahead. Number 2 tells us nothing about the particular unit except that it follows number 1 and precedes number 3. This militates against the individual standing of each unit. The only permissible counting would yield the information that there are [potentially] an infinite number of 1 (understood as "אחד" not as "ראשון").

5 ... כי טעם "במספר שמות" שיגידו כל אחד שמותם בפקוד אותם בכופר

6 ... הבט נא השמימה וראה אם תוכל לספור אותם

7 מונה מספר לככבים לכלם שמות יקרא.

8 The concept of הפקר בית דין הפקר is in no sense similar to the secular concept of Eminent Domain. The later grants the State a form of ownership over the individual's possessions:

The property of subjects is under the eminent *domain* of the state, so that the state or he who acts for it may use and even alienate and destroy such property... for ends of public utility, to which ends *those who founded civil society must be supposed to have intended that private ends should give way.*

NOTES

That is not the case in הפקר בית דין. It is not grounded in an overriding ownership but in the power that the Ribono shel Olam conferred upon Beis Din to expropriate property. (See, however, Rabbeinu Yonah quoted in Shitah Mekubetzes to Bava Basra 54b.) And, let us remember that presumably the power to be מפקיר is also conferred upon the judges as a part of their standing as שלוחים of the Ribono shel Olam.

9 See Tehilim 82:1.

10 I mean this in the sense that, as we have shown, every citizen in the *Mamleches Kohanim VeGoy Kadosh* is unique. He occupies a world of his own. In that world he is the Ribono shel Olam's only child.

NINETEEN *The Tenth* Dibra

1 אונאת דברים, לשון הרע, נקימה, נטירה וכו'.

2 In the Ramban that we are about to examine below (Shemos 20:13–14), there is a strange locution that may throw some light on this issue. In the section that is of interest to us at this point, Ramban discusses the sequence in which the *Dibros* are organized. After bringing us up to the seventh *Dibra* Ramban continues, ". . . after that we come to kidnapping, false testimony, and robbery." Now clearly "robbery" is meant to describe the tenth *Dibra, Lo tachmod*. Why describe an inappropriate importuning to gain an object to which one has no right as "robbery"? I have seen various commentators who raise the question, but have not found their answers particularly satisfying. I have a feeling that perhaps Ramban here is using a system that we can observe in Sefer Yechezkel, chapter 18. In that passage Yechezkel offers descriptions of the kinds of things that wicked people would do but that righteous people would eschew. One of those actions is described as "*defiling his neighbor's wife.*" Now it seems strange to us to classify someone who does not defile another's wife as a *tzadik*. It would seem to us that, in order to attain such an exalted standing, much more would be required than simply abstaining from a dastardly crime. Indeed Chazal in Sanhedrin 81a propose that the phrase "defiling his neighbor's wife" stands in for a quite different action. It is a metaphor for one who interferes with his neighbor's livelihood, perhaps opening a competing store where the circumstances are such that this would not be permitted.

This Gemara is generally understood to mean that undermining one's neighbor's business can likely be only a first step to violating his wife. Once my neighbor's possessions are not sacrosanct in my eyes, the rest is only a matter of degree.

If Ramban agrees with this explanation, it is possible that this insight guided his pen in the present instance. As we saw earlier in the Rambam that we quoted within, coveting someone's possessions can easily lead to robbing him. Following Yechezkel's daring locution, it is possible that coveting may be called "robbery" as easily as unfair competition can be described as adultery.

If all this is true, then our question as to why stealing does not rise to the level of a *Dibra* could be readily answered. It is, in fact, a *Dibra*, subsumed under *Lo tachmod*.

3 I obviously am not making a judgment about the relative values of the various *Dibros*. When I use the expression "pinnacle" I mean that, as the final *Dibra* of the ten, it may well have a unique function, as I will explain within.

4 Yiddish for "It is not fitting." It is not in accordance with the dignified bearing that is appropriate to your exalted status.

5 The time has come to fulfill our promise made in chapter 1, that in the course of the book we would define the terms *Mamleches Kohanim VeGoy Kadosh*.

Mamleches Kohanim is the more complex of the two. Rashi takes כהנים as שרים, *princes* or *aristocrats*. (For an elaboration of this idea, please turn to the final paragraphs of the book at the end of chapter 21.) Ramban disagrees and renders the term משרתים, *people who serve*. If you would like to have a more rounded view of how Ramban understands the term, I recommend that you take a few moments to study Ramban to Bereishis 41:45. There you will find that Ramban is closer to Rashi than would appear from the short remark that he makes here.

Ramban renders גוי קדוש as *a nation that cleaves to the Holy One*. In his view, reiterated in a number of places throughout his commentary, this term contains a promise for life after death.

6 אצילות מחייבת.

7 Earlier in this essay we pointed out that this connection requires some explaining. How does the one follow from the other? The thoughts that we have offered in the past few paragraphs provide the answer. Certainly if I do not covet because by nature I am a מסתפק במועט, *easily satisfied, unambitious*, there would be little logic to Ramban's statement. I may still be a careless driver and bump into your fenders. But if my satisfaction with my lot stems from my conviction that I own everything that I need because I believe firmly that the Ribono shel Olam will arrange things, what I own and what I do not own, in precisely the amounts that I require in order to serve Him best, then I will be acutely aware that what holds true for me holds true also for my neighbor. His situation too, the balance of what he has and has not, reflects precisely what the Ribono shel Olam has in store for him. Once I am convinced of that, I will be very, very careful not to damage him in any way.

8 The idea that Mishpatim teaches laws that are specifically designed for a *Mamleches Kohanim VeGoy Kadosh* and that would be illogical in any other setting is a major part of the theories that I have propounded in this book. It is an idea with which I have lived for some time now. Those of you who have read my book *Ramban as Guide to Today's Perplexed* may recall that in the Epilogue to that book I discussed a number of *mitzvos* in Mishpatim from that point of view. This subject is of such significance for the present book that I really should devote more pages to it than is possible given the

restraints of space. This book is already longer than it should be. I will devote the next chapter to the *mitzvah* of *eved Ivri* but that is about as far as I will be able to go. I really suggest for those of you who are as fascinated with this theory as I am, to read that Epilogue again if you have access to it.

TWENTY Parashas Mishpatim *and the* Eved Ivri

1 זמן מתן תורתנו.

2 My good friend R. Simchah Hexter has pointed out to me that the Beis HaLevi to Yisro deals with the same problem as I do here. His explanation differs completely from the one that I suggest here. I was delighted to discover that my question is a reasonable one and that others have been stimulated to think it through.

3 There are many passages in the *aggadah* literature that attempt to explain how Moshe Rabbeinu came to deserve that the Torah should be called "his" Torah. Mostly the explanations center about the fact that he sacrificed much for Torah (מסר נפשו עליה) and the like. Shabbos 89a offers his modesty (... הואיל ומיעטת עצמך) as the reason. For our purposes in this essay, the array of possible answers is less significant than the fact that an answer is necessary. The answers that are given are all indigenous to Moshe Rabbeinu. To the best of my knowledge there are no similar discussions concerning the "Torah of Israel." But then, as we have noted, this or similar phrases do not occur in TaNaCh.

4 זאת תורת הנזיר.

5 The situation is similar to the problem in *parashas* Naso in Sefer BeMidbar, where the narrative is also interrupted by the *parshiyos* of גזל הגר, סוטה, and נזיר. There Ramban, though not Rashi, finds himself called upon to explain how these seemingly intrusive halachic passages fit in.

6 Not אלה המשפטים but ואלה המשפטים.

7 This is the opinion of R. Akiva. The question of course arises that this threefold revelation of *all* the *mitzvos* is not reflected in the Torah's account. In the Torah text some *mitzvos* (for example, those contained in Mishpatim) are written as though they were taught *only* at Sinai; some (for example, all the sacrificial laws as taught in VaYikra), as though they were taught *only* from the Ohel Mo'ed; and some (for example all the new *mitzvos* in *parashas* Ki Seitzei) as though they were taught *only* in Arvos Moav.
The matter requires serious discussion but does not play a role in the issues upon which we are focused in this essay. For an important treatment, see Chazon Ish, Orech Chaim 125.

8 I am aware that before the מעשה עגל and the מרגלים, the expectation was that they would enter Eretz Yisrael much faster than they eventually did. Still, it is difficult to see what the urgency might have been. It seems that issues like שור, בור, מבעה, and הבער would have had immediate applications while they were still traveling, and should, so we would have thought, perhaps have been taught before *eved Ivri*.

9 The *sugios* that deal with *eved Ivri* know of two categories. One is called מוכר עצמו, a person who is completely destitute and must enter into servitude in order to be able to eat, and the other is מכרוהו בית דין, the case described within. The Gemara concludes that Mishpatim deals with the latter case while the *parshah* of *eved Ivri* in BeHar speaks of the מוכר עצמו.

10 I use "cohabit" because there cannot be a legal marriage between a Jew and a שפחה כנענית.

11 I use "non-Jewish" in its literal sense. The slave girl is not "Jewish." עבדים כנענים and שפחות כנעניות have a kind of intermediate status. When they become עבדים or שפחות they go through a partial גרות that obligates them in certain *mitzvos*.

12 If you want to do yourself a favor, look at the Hirsch commentary to Mishpatim. Among other things he points out that the license for the *eved* to cohabit with a שפחה כנענית legalizes a purely physical relationship, in no way sanctified by marital ties.
He understands the six years of servitude to which the *eved* is bound as being related to the six days of Creation and the six years of work in the fields until the sanctifying שמיטה comes along. There are many who see the number six as projecting the six directions of physicality (up, down, and the four compass points). The symbolism is clear. The *eved* is told that for the period of his עבדות, he is entangled in pure physicality. Witness his license to cohabit with the שפחה. He must await the vivifying redemption, which the seventh year (his private Shabbos, his private Shemitah) will bring to him, to be reinstated into the world of the spirit.

13 עבד עברי עובד בין ביום ובין בלילה (Kidushin 15a).

TWENTY-ONE *Some Answers to Some Significant Questions*

1 The exception is Binyamin who was born after the name change had already taken place. However, we should remember that Binyamin, by calling all his ten sons by names that recalled episodes from Yoseph's life, seemed to affirm that, in real terms, he viewed himself as an extension of Yosef rather than as a discrete "*shevet*" personality.
By the sheerest chance, if there is such a thing, I happened to glance at Bereishis 49:2 about five minutes after I wrote the above paragraph. There Yaakov adjures his sons as בני יעקב to listen to what their father, ישראל, was about to tell them. There I saw the following sentence in the רביני בחיי:

הקבצו ושמעו הזכיר להם ב' שמותיו יעקב וישראל, והזכיר הבנים אצל יעקב כי בזמן שהיה שמו יעקב היו לו הבנים.

This confirms the suggestion that I made within.
As far as the switch from "Yaakov" to "Yisrael" in this verse is concerned, it can be readily explained on the basis of what I have written within. When he called to his sons, intent upon giving them his final blessing, he addressed them as בני יעקב; he wanted them to look upon themselves as one family. However, since what he was about to do was to point out to them that,

within this community, it was still possible to maintain a separate *shevet* identity—witness the fact that he very clearly differentiated among them by giving each one a clearly defined blessing, appropriate only to him—he used "Yisrael" because that name had become his, when he had affirmed his own individuality. See the following note.

2 I am of course aware that the terms בית ישראל and בני ישראל are to be found, spread far and wide, throughout TaNaCh. However, I believe that in that context "Yisrael" is not used to describe the third patriarch but that it is simply the name of the Jewish people. There are several sources for this contention. The locus classicus is Bereishis 46:8, where the שבעים נפש associated with Yaakov's descent into Egypt are introduced. The verses reads, ואלה שמות **בני ישראל** הבאים מצרימה . . . . Now there are numerous commentators, beginning with Rashbam, who believe that Yaakov himself was included in the count of seventy. That given, it transpires that Yaakov is described as part of the בני ישראל. That, of course, is only possible if the meaning of "בני ישראל" is as I have now suggested. (If you want to follow up on this Rashbam, I suggest that you learn his comments to Bereishis 46:8, with particular emphasis on what he says concerning verse 15. After that, please move to the Rashbam on verse 27.)

See also Rabbeinu Bechaya to Bereishis 46:8, who maintains that we find the name "Yisrael" attached to each of the three patriarchs. For Avraham he cites ומושב בני ישראל אשר ישבו בארץ מצרים . . . . Now it is well known that in the tradition of Chazal this dating of the Egyptian exile begins with Yitzchak's birth. The "Yisrael" in the phrase "בני ישראל" must therefore refer to Avraham. For Yitzchak he cites the description that Chazal use for Eisav: ישראל מומר. "ישראל" there must refer to Yitzchak.

3 אלהי נצור לשוני מרע . . .

4 We should note that, in addition, we introduce our תפילה with ה' שפתי תפתח . . . and end with יהיו לרצון אמרי פי . . . , both of which are couched in the singular.

5 And, let us remember that Yaakov Avinu, the only one of the Avos explicitly associated with studying Torah in the academy of Shem and Ever, did so specifically while he was on his way to find a mate with whom he would be destined to build the nation of Israel. It is in the context of incipient nationhood that he first received the Torah.

6 It is possible that our rather convoluted effort to find different meanings for "Yaakov" and "Yisrael" was not necessary according to Ramban. At Bereishis 46:2 he points out that when we are strong, fighters who are able to challenge even the angels, we are called "Yisrael". But when we descend to "Egypt" destined for slavery, we are "Yaakov."

7 כה תאמר לבית יעקב.

8 ותגד לבני ישראל.

9 זכות הרבים.

10 See Mishnah Berurah to Orech Chayim 591:17.

11 Based on Mishnah, Ta'anis 4:8. Perhaps at this point you might wish to glance back at chapters 8 and 9.

12 Bava Basra 75a. זקנים שבאותו הדור אמרו פני משה כפני חמה פני יהושע כפני לבנה.

13 אנכי עמד **בין** יהוה וביניכם.

14 Ramban at Devarim 14:14 suggests that האמרת in our passage does not derive from the root אמר, *to say*, but from an independent root אמר, also sometimes written עמר, from which the noun אמיר, the crown of the tree (See Yeshayahu 17:6) derives. Thus we have *to lift up* or *to exalt*. This etymological exercise ignores Rashi on our passage who can find no analogy for האמרת, and, from the context in which it appears, surmises that it expresses the idea of *separation*.

15 See chapter 1, note 5.

16 It is worthy of note that here in Sefer Devarim, our exaltation of the Ribono shel Olam precedes His exaltation of us. This is in contrast to the beginning of VaEirah in Sefer Shemos where ולקחתי אתכם לי לעם precedes והייתי לכם לאלהים. There the Ribono shel Olam takes the initiative; here it is we who begin the process. The explanation is, of course, that at the beginning of the desert experience we were Jewishly illiterate. We were not in a position to choose to make the Ribono shel Olam our God because, after two centuries of slavery (dogged by constant idol worship—see Yechezkel, chapter 20), we simply lacked the religious sophistication to make such a choice. God had to step into our history and, as it were, introduce Himself to us. The rest then followed.

Things were different after forty years of desert wandering. Once we had received, and willingly accepted, the entire Torah, we knew very well what we were called upon to do. When the Ribono shel Olam saw how unquestioningly we subordinated ourselves to Him, He reciprocated by granting us a glimpse of what lay in store for us if we but managed to stick with our resolve.

17 Here Beis HaYayin references Devarim 4:6–7.

18 For this phrase and the next, I have borrowed from Rav Chavel's translation.

19 Here Beis HaYayin references Devarim 4:6–7.

20 See chapter 2.

21 There is, of course, the unforgettable Rashi to this *pasuk*. Here is a paraphrase:

What I did to Mitzrayim: Long before you were involved with the Egyptians they had committed enough sins to have me punish them. I never did anything about it because they were of no importance to Me. Only once they were cruel to you, did I release all My wrath against them.

The message is one of love and caring. The earlier wickedness of the Egyptians meant nothing to Me. They attracted My enmity only because they began to bother you. You see how much I love you and care for you. You will now understand that whatever I will demand of you will be nothing else than an expression of that love.

All this, however, is clearly not included in the *p'shuto shel mikra*.

22 אתם ראיתם את אשר עשיתי למצרים, ואשא אתכם על כנפי נשרים, **ואביא אתכם אלי**.

23 Here is Ramban's language: אל מקום כבודי ההר הזה אשר שכינתי שם **עמכם**.

24 I am making the point that the Ribono shel Olam does not say that He undertook all that He did so that He might be able to give us the Torah. He stresses the closeness that was to become the defining feature of the relationship between Him and us. We have argued that Matan Torah was a function of that relationship.

25 See chapter 19, note 8.

לזכר נשמת

ר' מרדכי דוד

בן ר' יצחק יעקב ז"ל

דינוביץ

איש תם וישר

יליד ירושלים וחניכה

הוקיר רבנן

פעל להחזקת התורה

אהוב אהב ולעמו דאג

"עושה צדקות בכל עת"

נפטר בן צ"א שנים ביום כ' סיון תשס"ז

IN RECOGNITION OF A

GENEROUS CONTRIBUTION

IN MEMORY

OF

Dr. Richard

&

Regina Weinberger

OF

VIENNA, AUSTRIA

AND

BALTIMORE, MARYLAND

IN MEMORY

OF

OUR BELOVED

HUSBAND, FATHER,

AND

TEACHER

Solomon Ralph Bijou

HE LIT A LIGHT IN OUR HEARTS

THAT

WILL GUIDE US AND OUR CHILDREN

THROUGHOUT OUR LIVES.

—FROM HIS WIFE,

CHILDREN, GRANDCHILDREN,

AND

GREAT-GRANDCHILDREN

IN LOVING MEMORY

OF

Esther & Isaac Mezrahi

PILLARS OF OUR COMMUNITY,

THEY ALWAYS KNEW WHAT HAD TO BE DONE

AND, PROFOUNDLY CREATIVE,

FOUND WAYS TO DO IT.

ABOVE ALL THEY WERE A TEAM.

ONE HEART

ANIMATED THEM BOTH,

ONE SOUL

BREATHED LIFE INTO THEIR DREAMS.

AFTER FATHER PASSED ON,

MOTHER KEPT THE FLAME BURNING

FOR EIGHTEEN MORE YEARS.

MAY THEIR MEMORY BE A BLESSING

FOR US, OUR CHILDREN, AND GRANDCHILDREN.

THERE ARE MANY PEOPLE

WHO OWE

THEIR LIVES

TO

THE LOVING CONCERN OF

Ezra & Zekia Shasho

OF BLESSED MEMORY.

WE GRATEFULLY RECALL THEIR GOODNESS AND

THE WONDERFUL EXAMPLE THAT THEY SET.

THEY, AS ALSO

THEIR BELOVED DAUGHTER

Frieda Kredy

OF BLESSED MEMORY,

WILL FOREVER LIVE ON IN OUR HEARTS.

—BY THEIR CHILDREN,

GRANDCHILDREN, AND FAMILY

Albert Hamway זצ"ל

UNDERSTOOD WHAT JEWISH LIVING

WAS ALL ABOUT.

IN FARAWAY JAPAN HE RAISED HIS CHILDREN

WITH A LOVE FOR THEIR TRADITION.

THEY EACH BUILT

WARM AND LOVING JEWISH HOMES,

PASSING ON TO THEIR CHILDREN AND

THEY TO THEIRS THE FLAME

WHICH THEIR FATHER HAD PASSED TO THEM.

HE IS REMEMBERED WITH LOVE BY

HIS WIFE, HIS CHILDREN,

GRANDCHILDREN,

AND GREAT-GRANDCHILDREN.

מציבים אנו בזה

מזכרת נצח

לאבינו מורנו היקר

ר' לטמן

בן ר' חיים דוב בער ז"ל

איש צנוע

שכל חייו רץ כצבי

לעשות רצון אבינו שבשמים

ולאמנו מורתנו היקרה

רות רבקה לאה

בת ר' אברהם ע"ה

יהא זכרם ברוך

IN LOVING MEMORY

OF

OUR PARENTS

Mollie

AND

Sam E. Levy

*

IN LOVING MEMORY

OF MY BELOVED PARENTS,

AND

MORE, MY GOOD AND PRECIOUS

FRIENDS

Jack & Jeanette Feldman

THEY WERE GENEROUS, WARMHEARTED,

AND GENTLE.

YOU COULD NOT MEET THEM

WITHOUT BEING TOUCHED BY THEIR

GOODNESS.

WITH A SMILE ON HIS WISE FACE

AND NOVHARDOK MUSSAR IN HIS HEART

HaRav
Chaim Mordechai
Weinkrantz זצ"ל

UNDERSTOOD US ALL SO WELL, SO VERY WELL.

NO PROBLEM,

BUT HIS WISDOM FOUND A SOLUTION.

NO PAIN, BUT HIS EMPATHY

WAS A HEALING BALM.

CHILD OF A CULTURE VERY DIFFERENT

FROM OUR OWN, HE NEVERTHELESS FOUND

COMMONALITY IN HIS AND OUR

JEWISH HEARTS.

WE WILL NEVER FORGET THE BOOKS

WHICH HE SO DILIGENTLY TAUGHT US,

NOR THE LIFE LESSONS

FOR WHICH HE WAS A LIVING TEXT.

—THE MONDAY SHIUR